A Beginner's Guide to
OVERLOCKERS, SERGERS & COVERLOCKERS

50 lessons & 15 projects to get you started

Clémentine Lubin

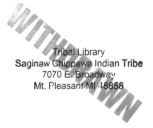

SEARCH PRESS

Contents

Lessons

Introduction

WHAT IS AN OVERLOCKER?

‣ It is a machine that trims, stitches and overlocks in a single action. As the fabric passes under the presser foot, and before it reaches the needles, a 'cutter' blade trims the fabric cleanly. Approximately 5mm (¼in) further on, a needle (or two needles) stitches through the layers and another overlocks the edges in a single action.
The resulting seam is very neat.

‣ This 'overlock' stitch is also suitable for stretch fabric as it stretches, too (see pages 28-29).

‣ A particular function specific to this type of machine, known as differential feed, allows the fabric's elasticity to be gathered or stretched. This means seams are much neater and finishings more professional.

WHAT IS A SERGER?

A serger does the same job as an overlocker and is very similar, but in addition it may have more spools of thread, enabling it to perform more decorative stitches than just the overlock stitch. For the purposes of this book, we will just refer to the overlocker, but the same job may be done by a serger.

USER GUIDE
‣ Before using the overlocker, thread the 'loopers' (the upper looper passes over the fabric and the lower looper under the fabric) and the needles. To simplify this stage, there is a colour-coded threading diagram on the inside cover of the machine, and coloured stickers on the thread guides (see page 8 for a labelled photograph).

‣ Next, thread the needles, following the same colour code (first the right needle, then the left needle).

‣ The tension of each thread is adjusted separately. Unlike a conventional domestic sewing machine, threads of different kinds can be used for a single seam.

‣ The fabric feeds through an overlocker much more quickly than a conventional sewing machine. An overlocker is used in addition to, rather than in replacement of, a conventional sewing machine, as it can only be used for seams along the edge of fabric.

‣ The projects in this book have been made using three machines from different ranges that are described on the following pages.

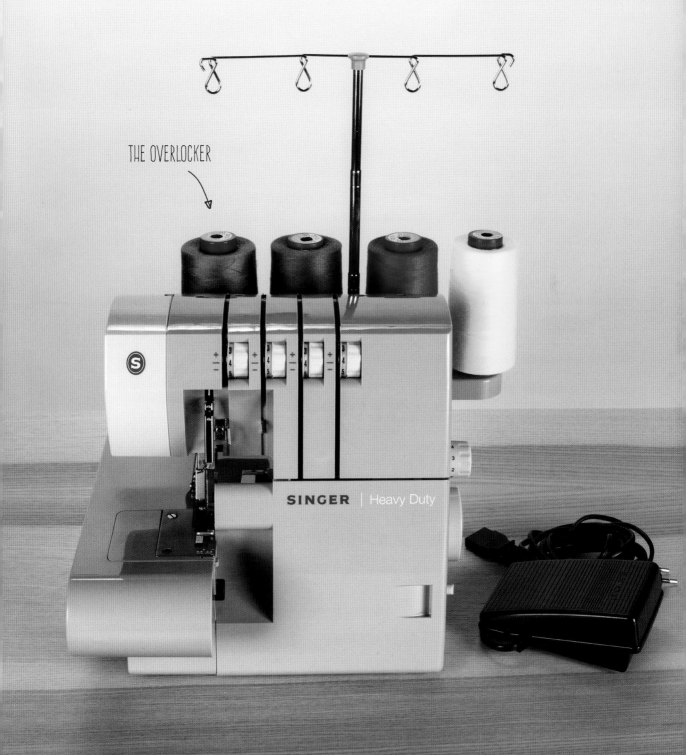

THE OVERLOCKER

SINGER | Heavy Duty

Introduction

WHAT IS A COVERLOCKER?

It is useful for:
- sewing hems on stretch fabrics, using coverstitch
- solid stitching on thick fabric using chain stitch.

TECHNICAL FEATURES

› **Coverstitch is sewn using two or three needles** that sew a straight stitch on the right side of the fabric. On the wrong side, a thread through a single looper forms big loops which conceal and coverlock the edge of the fabric. This seam is stretchy: garments can be stretched when being put on and taken off without the risk of the seams tearing or making holes (see page 30).

› **Chain stitch** is formed by positioning a single needle (in the middle) and stitching with the looper thread. This stitch is solid and slightly stretchy. It is very decorative when sewn on the wrong side with fancy thread (see page 30).

WHAT IS AN OVERLOCKER–COVERLOCKER?

› This is a combination machine that creates overlock stitches (overlocking/serging) and hems (coverlocking) as well as chain stitch. It is not possible to overlock and coverlock at the same time as the two actions are very different.

› The machine needs to be configured differently when you swap from one action to the other. Swapping from overlocking to coverlocking is explained in Lesson 32, page 116.

› The combi overlocker–coverlocker creates a stitch known as the '5-thread safety stitch', which produces an ultra-solid chain stitch at the same time as overlocking the hem. Only 5-thread machines give this option (see page 28).

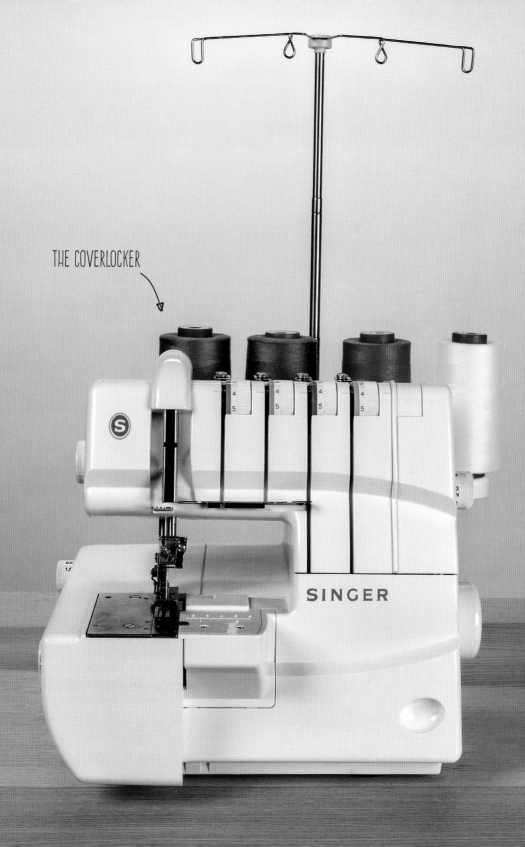

THE COVERLOCKER

Introduction

THE BASIC OVERLOCKER

1. Thread-guide
2. Carry handle
3. Left needle thread tension dial (blue)
4. Right needle thread tension dial (green)
5. Upper looper thread tension dial (red)
6. Lower looper thread tension dial (yellow)
7. Needle plate
8. Cloth plate
9. Looper cover
10. Power switch
11. Hand wheel
12. Stitch length dial
13. Spool holder
14. Presser bar
15. Differential feed adjusting lever knob
16. Seam width finger support plate
17. Threading diagram
18. Removable arm

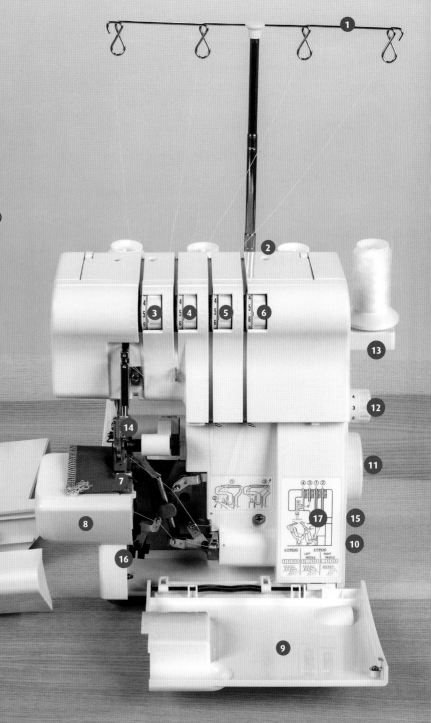

WHO IS IT FOR?

‣ The simplest, most basic model is perfect for beginners.

WHAT IS IT FOR?

‣ The machine cuts, stitches and overlocks with 3 or 4 threads on stretch or non-stretch fabrics. Like all overlockers, it can only be used for hems.
‣ It stitches 3- or 4-thread overlocks, rolled hems and decorative flatlock and pin tucks. It also sews blind hems.

TECHNICAL FEATURES

‣ The machine has two needle threads, an upper looper and a lower looper.
‣ Its removable arm is very practical for tubular seams (attaching collars).
‣ The movable cutter can be disengaged.
‣ The presser foot pressure can be adjusted.
‣ There are two stitch widths depending on the needle position: the left needle gives a wider overlock than the right needle.
‣ Stitch length can be adjusted.

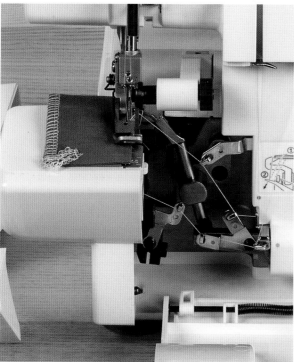

Advantages

The stitch-type table in your machine's instruction manual will give recommended tension settings. These are a good starting point for beginners. The machine is sold with four spools of white thread pre-threaded. This means you can give stitching and overlocking a go before changing the thread. The machine is compact and does not take up much storage room.

Introduction

THE HEAVY-DUTY OVERLOCKER

1. Thread-guide
2. Handle
3. Left needle thread tension dial (blue)
4. Right needle thread tension dial (green)
5. Upper looper thread tension dial (pink)
6. Lower looper thread tension dial (yellow)
7. Needle plate
8. Removable arm
9. Looper cover
10. Power switch
11. Hand wheel
12. Stitch length dial
13. Spool holder
14. Presser bar
15. Differential feed adjusting lever knob
16. Seam width finger support plate
17. Threading diagram

Accessories
18. Scrap bag
19. Threading tweezers
20. Screwdriver
21. Cleaning brush
22. Needles
23. Cutter
24. Spreader
25. Control pedal

WHO IS IT FOR?
› This would make a good first overlocker for the occasional dressmaker.

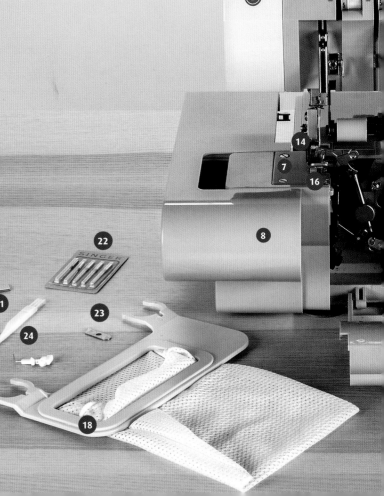

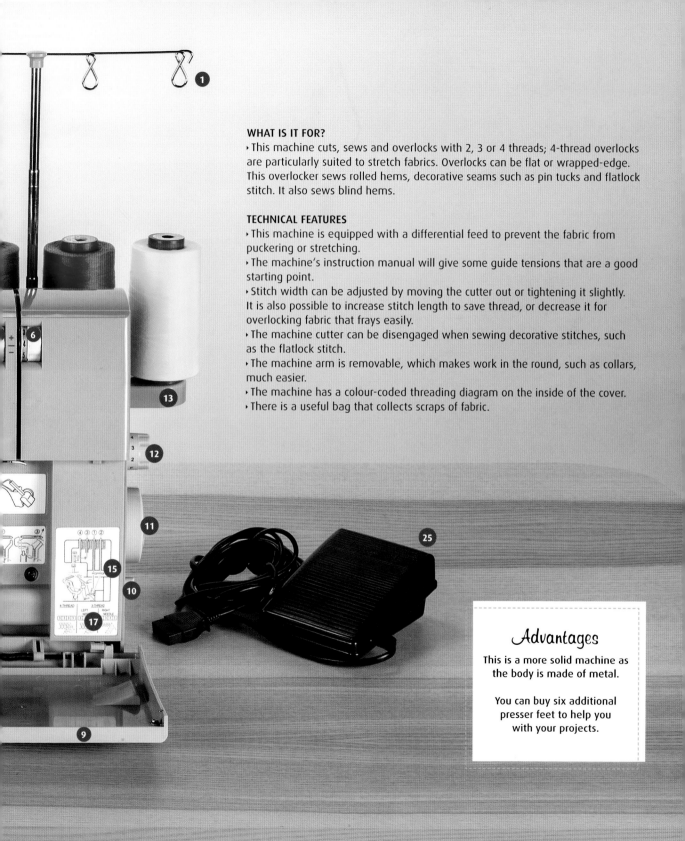

WHAT IS IT FOR?

‣ This machine cuts, sews and overlocks with 2, 3 or 4 threads; 4-thread overlocks are particularly suited to stretch fabrics. Overlocks can be flat or wrapped-edge. This overlocker sews rolled hems, decorative seams such as pin tucks and flatlock stitch. It also sews blind hems.

TECHNICAL FEATURES

‣ This machine is equipped with a differential feed to prevent the fabric from puckering or stretching.
‣ The machine's instruction manual will give some guide tensions that are a good starting point.
‣ Stitch width can be adjusted by moving the cutter out or tightening it slightly. It is also possible to increase stitch length to save thread, or decrease it for overlocking fabric that frays easily.
‣ The machine cutter can be disengaged when sewing decorative stitches, such as the flatlock stitch.
‣ The machine arm is removable, which makes work in the round, such as collars, much easier.
‣ The machine has a colour-coded threading diagram on the inside of the cover.
‣ There is a useful bag that collects scraps of fabric.

Advantages

This is a more solid machine as the body is made of metal.

You can buy six additional presser feet to help you with your projects.

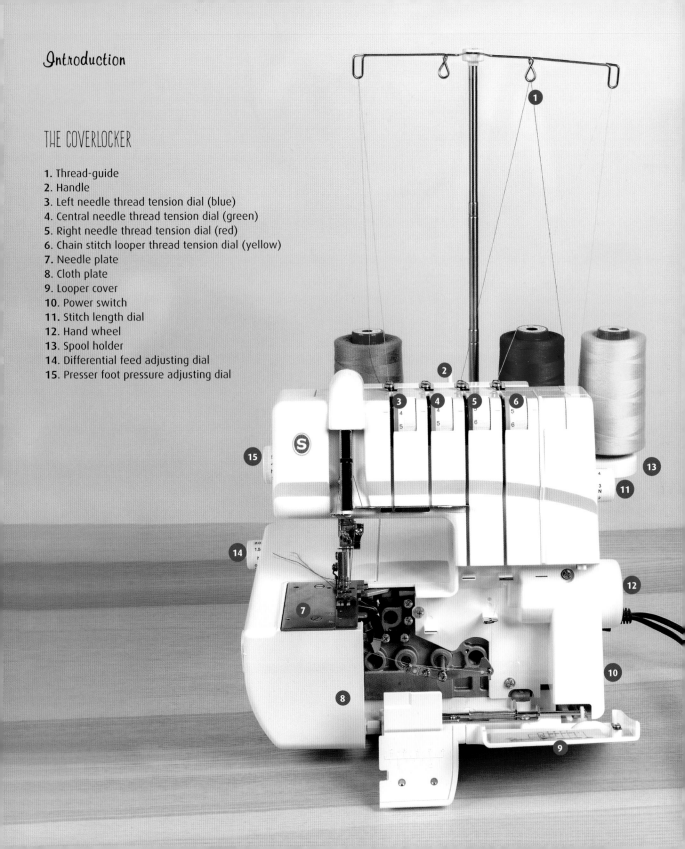

Introduction

THE COVERLOCKER

1. Thread-guide
2. Handle
3. Left needle thread tension dial (blue)
4. Central needle thread tension dial (green)
5. Right needle thread tension dial (red)
6. Chain stitch looper thread tension dial (yellow)
7. Needle plate
8. Cloth plate
9. Looper cover
10. Power switch
11. Stitch length dial
12. Hand wheel
13. Spool holder
14. Differential feed adjusting dial
15. Presser foot pressure adjusting dial

WHO IS IT FOR?
‣ If you already have an overlocker, this machine makes a good addition for stitching hems.

WHAT IS IT FOR?
‣ This machine sews coverstitch and chain stitch.

‣ Coverstitch is useful for hemming items made from stretch fabric. You can sew a narrow coverstitch (two close needles), wide coverstitch (two needles set further apart) or triple coverstitch (three needles), as well as chain stitch.

‣ The coverlocker produces chain stitch much more quickly than a conventional sewing machine. It is also much more solid. It is used to stitch curtains and bags made from heavy fabrics.

TECHNICAL FEATURES
The Singer 14 T 870 C coverlocker has a differential feed that enables you to produce neat seams on stretch fabric. Coverlockers do not have cutters because the fabric is folded before being stitched to produce an attractive hem.

Advantages
The machine's instruction manual contains a handy reference table for each stitch suggesting tension settings.

Introduction

THE COMBINATION MACHINE

1. Thread-guide
2. Carry handle
3. Left needle thread tension fine tuning lever (yellow)
4. Central needle thread tension fine tuning lever (blue)
5. Upper looper thread tension fine tuning lever (green)
6. Lower looper thread tension fine tuning lever (pink)
7. Chain stitch looper thread tension fine tuning lever (red)
8. Needle plate
9. Cloth plate
10. Looper cover
11. Power switch
12. Stitch length dial
13. Hand wheel
14. Automatic stitch-tension adjustment dial (ATD)

Photograph opposite
15. Presser foot pressure adjusting dial
16. Differential feed adjusting dial
17. Cutting width dial
18. Presser bar
19. Stitch finger
20. Removable cover
21. Automatic tension adjustment diagram

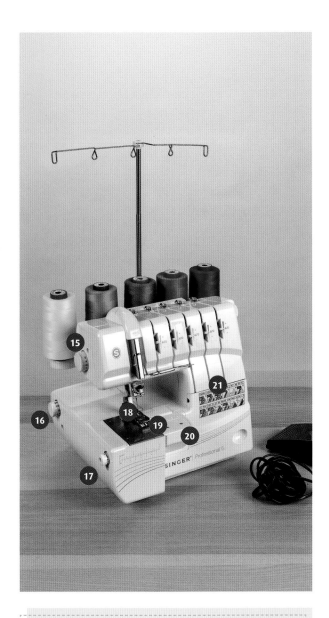

Note for beginners

It is not possible to use all five needles at the same time because the settings and stitches are very different. It can be used either as an overlocker or a coverlocker.

WHO IS IT FOR?

‣ This model is recommended if you don't have much storage room at home (it is a 'combi').
‣ Ideal for anyone who has already mastered using an overlocker.

WHAT IS IT FOR?

‣ The overlocker-coverlocker overlocks stretch or non-stretch fabric with 2, 3, 4 or 5 threads. It produces very neat, coverlocked hems. It sews very fast chain stitch on heavy fabrics.
‣ It can sew 14 different stitches; overlocks rolled hems, decorative stitches such as pin tucks and flatlocks and, of course, coverstitch. It can sew blind hems.

TECHNICAL FEATURES

‣ This model has all the features of an overlocker combined with those of a coverlocker. You have to change the machine's settings to swap between the two (see page 116).
‣ It has two needles for overlocking, three needles for coverlocking and three loopers.
‣ The movable cutter can be disengaged.
‣ It has a differential feed, meaning that the fabric's elasticity can be gathered or stretched during stitching.
‣ Stitch width and length can be adjusted. Presser foot pressure can be adjusted.
‣ It has a waste tray to collect scraps of fabric.
‣ There is a colour-coded threading guide inside the looper cover. A reminder of automatic tension settings is given on the front of the machine.
‣ The user manual specifies which needles and which automatic tension setting should be used for each stitch you are using and provides troubleshooting if it is not properly adjusted.
‣ You can buy six additional presser feet to help with your projects.

Advantages

The 5-thread coverlocking and overlocking stitch option is a big plus point. The machine has the enormous advantage of automatically regulating thread tension. This machine has a safety feature: it will not stitch if the cover is open (this means you can use the light for threading!).

HOW DOES IT DIFFER FROM A CONVENTIONAL SEWING MACHINE?

‣ An overlocker and coverlocker would be used in addition to a conventional sewing machine. You would still use a normal sewing machine to sew darts, collars, cuffs and any seams that are not hems.

• Your conventional sewing machine may appear very simple... but also very slow compared to the overlocker!

‣ The following points will give you a better understanding of how the three machines complement each other:

- **(1, left)** an overlocked hem stitched on the overlocker. The edge is very neat. The fabric is well distributed. The stitching will not move. The four threads are visible.

- **(1, right)** a hem stitched with a conventional sewing machine. Three separate processes have been involved: cutting the fabric, sewing the two layers together, then overlocking with a zigzag stitch. This is much more fiddly and time consuming.

‣ **(2)** Hems do not stretch. Not suitable for jersey fabric.

‣ **(3)** Hems, like the fabric, are stretchy.

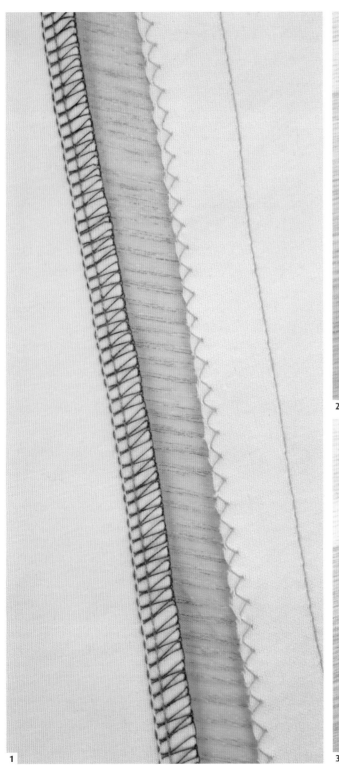

NEW CONCEPTS SPECIFIC TO OVERLOCKERS

Some terms are specific to overlockers.

OVERLOCK
Name of the stitch produced by the overlocker.

DIFFERENTIAL FEED
‣ The overlocker is fitted with two fabric feed dogs (as opposed to one on sewing machines): the back dog and front dog. The dogs are independent and are controlled by a dial. When the dial is set to 1 (or N) the dogs move at the same speed and the seam will be normal. This setting is used for non-stretch fabrics. When the dial is set to more than 1, the front feed dogs will move more quickly than the back feed dogs. When the dial is set to less than 1, the front feed dogs will move more slowly than the back feed dogs. This means the fabric's elasticity can be gathered or stretched.

INTERESTING FACT
The early overlockers did not have a differential feed. It was the presser foot, feeding the fabric through at a lesser or greater speed, which provided the differential.

THREAD TENSION
‣ Each thread has its own specific tension adjustment, which makes it possible to sew with different sorts of threads (see page 26).

CHAINING OFF
‣ All hems stitched on an overlocker start with sewing a thread chain. This allows you to check that:
- the threads are feeding correctly
- they are working well together, taking into account any necessary tension adjustments.

(2) *Rolled chain stitch.*

(1) *Sewing an elastic stretch fabric with a differential feed of 0.8.* **1**

2

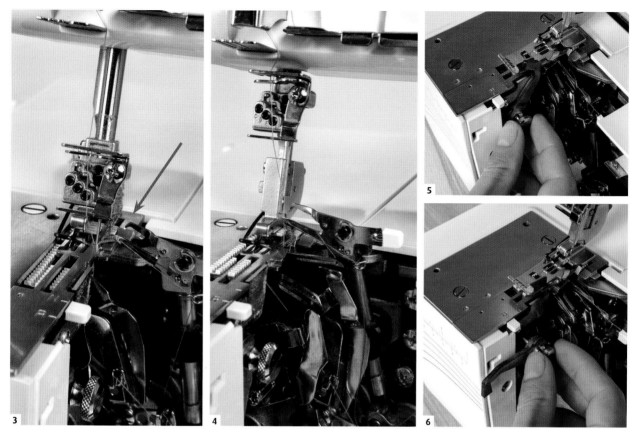

(3) *Position N (Neutral) or S (Overlock) (depending on model).*
(4) *Position R or rolled.*

THE STITCH FINGER
› This is a small, retractable metal part mounted under the pressure foot.
- By activating the stitch finger in position N (for Neutral) or S (for Overlock), the overlock will form under the pressure foot, around the stitch finger.
- The R stitch (for Rolled) is finer so the stitch finger should be retracted.

ENGAGING OR DISENGAGING THE CUTTER
› This applies to the overlocker only. Coverlockers do not have a cutter.
- The overlocker is fitted with a cutter (generally retractable), which trims the fabric just before it passes under the presser foot. Certain stitches, like the overlock, require the cutter to be activated **(5)**; for others, like flatlock or pin tucks, the fabric must not be trimmed.
- In these cases the cutter should be retracted **(6)**.

NEEDLE POSITION
There are two rows of needles:
- one front row for coverlockers
- one back row for overlockers.
Needle position will vary depending on the stitch.
The instruction manuals will give needle position.

THE TENSION DEVICE
› This is a removable part that is clicked into place on overlockers when only one looper is being used (i.e. for a 2-thread overlock). This stitch requires the second looper to be blocked with the tension device.

THE CONVERTER (only on the 5-thread model)
› This switches the machine from overlocker to coverlocker. You need to follow a series of steps.

Introduction

SEWING-BOX ACCESSORIES FOR OVERLOCKERS

‣ The accessories you need for overlockers and coverlockers are not very different from those you would use with a conventional sewing machine. The basics are the same.

‣ When you buy the machine a few specific tools will be provided – don't lose them!

1. A small screwdriver that fits the needle retainer screws

2. A replacement cutter for the overlocker

3. Spool caps

4. Anti-spill cone nets

5. Machine oil

6. A small screwdriver that goes with the machine

7. Threading tweezers

8. A set of needles

9. A small brush for removing lint

10. Cone adaptors

11. Storage box

12. Looper cover (for machines adaptable to coverstitching)

13. Small sewing scissors

‣ A few other accessories are worth having:
  - Seam binding: it will make life easier if you get a few metres (yards) in advance, in black or white
  - Thread cones (see 'Thread' section, page 26)

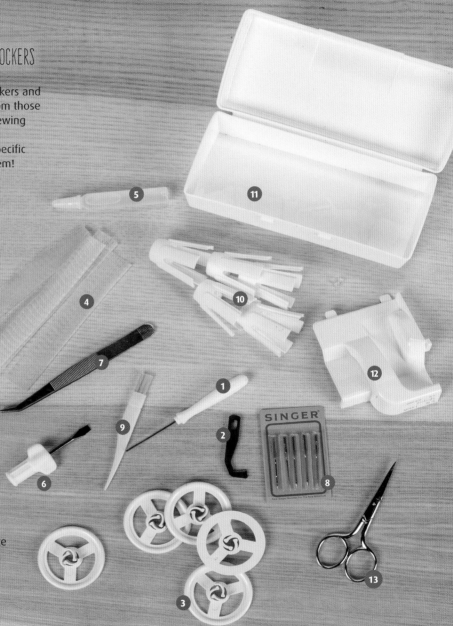

CLASSIC SEWING-BOX ACCESSORIES (THE BASICS)

1. A pair of sewing scissors (do not use this pair for anything other than cutting fabric and thread)
2. Small clips for keeping the fabric together
3. Needles
4. A few good quality safety pins for threading elastic and turning out bands
5. A tape measure

6. White tailor's chalk (for dark fabrics), or
7. A water-soluble fabric marker pen
8. An unpicker
9. Reels of thread
10. Tacking needles

Worth knowing

Note that pins are not compatible with these machines. If you leave one in by mistake, you might damage the cutter and the machine. Small clips are a perfect alternative.

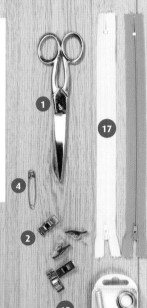
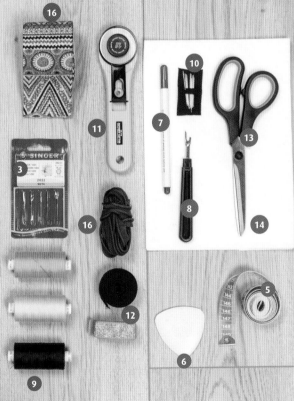

11. A rotary cutter for cutting in a straight line
12. Elastic

‣ Some suitable paper for copying patterns (which means you keep the originals intact)
13. A pencil case with marker pens and a pair of scissors
14. Pattern paper

‣ It is always a good idea to have a supply of the following, often left over from previous projects:
15. Eyelets
16. Coloured ribbon, piping
17. Zip fasteners
And also
- Snap fasteners
- Buttons
- A flat ruler

Tip

Try and make yourself a pleasant work space where you can leave the sewing machine (for all your day-to-day sewing needs), the overlocker and the coverlocker permanently at the ready. Ensure the machines are on a stable table. Have your fabrics and sewing basket close to hand. Have an iron nearby if possible – good seams need ironing.

OVERLOCKER PRESSER FEET

Different varieties of presser feet are sold separately. You don't necessarily need them, but they make life easier.

1. BEADING OR SEQUIN FOOT
If you like adding beaded binding, this will ensure it is well positioned in relation to the needles.

2. ELASTIC FOOT
The upper, adjustable screw means you can adjust the contraction of the elastic as you attach it to the garment.

3. SHIRRING FOOT
This foot allows you to sew two fabrics together while only gathering the fabric placed against the differential feed dogs.

4. WELTING OR CORDING FOOT
For sewing welting or piping between two pieces of fabric.

5. PIPING FOOT
For attaching piping. It will keep the piping well positioned in relation to the needles so it is not cut by the cutter.

6. BLIND HEM FOOT
The small cleat positions the edge of the fabric just a millimetre ($1/16$in) away from the needles.

> ## Worth knowing
>
> There is no foot for attaching zips, as they are laid edge to edge with the fabric. Machines are sold with a universal presser foot. The presser foot for the 4- to 5-thread model cannot be used on other models and vice versa.
>
> Coverlockers do not have specific presser feet.

NEEDLES

‣ Needles have specific references depending on the brand. Always use needles of the same brand as your machine, as recommended by the manufacturer. One side of the needle shank is flat. Overlock and/or coverlock needles are different from conventional sewing machine needles.

‣ Even a tiny difference in needle length can make sewing impossible, just as with a conventional sewing machine. Loops will not form correctly.

‣ Needles should be changed regularly. It is always worth buying several sets of needles in advance, especially as you will use several at a time. They are not expensive. By way of a guide, you need to change the needle after approximately every eight hours of use. If you know that the point is blunt, change it earlier! If you don't, the thread can break or snarl up the looping. If a thread breaks frequently as you sew, check your needle.

‣ The number represents the diameter of the needle: a classic 80 needle has a diameter of 0.8mm.
- For average fabrics, use 80 needles.
- For thin or light fabrics, use 70 needles.
- For very heavy fabrics (denim, canvas) use 90 needles.

‣ The machines listed all use Singer 2022 needles. The shanks are orange for thicker needles (90) and blue for the most commonly used (80).

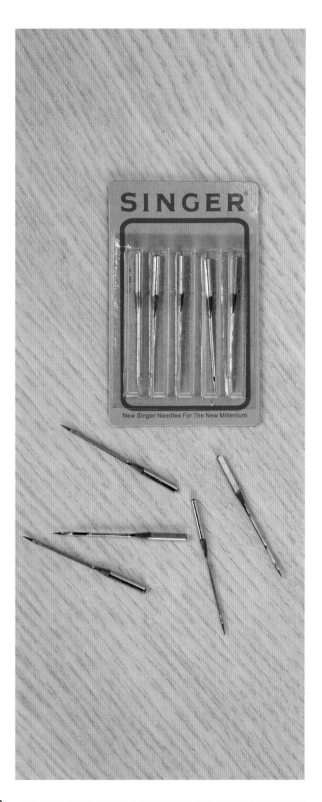

FABRICS

With overlockers you can sew all types of fabric together.

MATERIALS

1. NON-STRETCH FABRICS: these include cotton, twill, gabardine and denim. The overlocker sews these fabrics together very neatly and gives a nice finish to clothes and accessories.

2. VERY STRETCHY WOOLLEN FABRICS: difficult to put together with a conventional sewing machine. This type of fabric can be sewn very quickly and neatly on an overlocker. The overlock finish ensures the fabric can't fray or unravel.

3. JERSEY-STYLE STRETCH FABRICS: the stretch will not be the same in both directions. Overlockers are perfect for working with these materials. The elasticity of overlocked seams means they will not tear. Coverlockers make a neat, stretchy hem.

4. FAUX FUR AND MATERIALS THAT FRAY: a tight overlock is particularly suited to these fabrics.

5. VERY STRETCHY MATERIAL ON CUFFS AND HEMS: the elasticity of overlocked seams (4-thread, for example) is essential when working with this type of fabric.

WEIGHT

The weight of the fabric is important when choosing which stitch to use, adjusting presser foot pressure and selecting needle diameter:

- **FINE FABRICS** will be overlocked with a 2-thread overlock using a fine needle. Ease off presser foot pressure so as not to tear the fabric.

- **AVERAGE WEIGHT FABRICS** are the most commonly used. Sew together using a 3- or 4-thread overlock stitch and standard 80 needles.

- **THICK, HEAVY FABRICS** should be sewn together using a 4-thread overlock, or a 5-thread safety overlock, with a larger diameter needle (90) for greater firmness. These fabrics have a tendency to slip, so you need to put more pressure on the presser foot to keep them in place.

GRAIN OF THE FABRIC

The stretch of the fabric is not the same in both directions. As a result, you might have to adjust the differential. This is a task that will become very important.

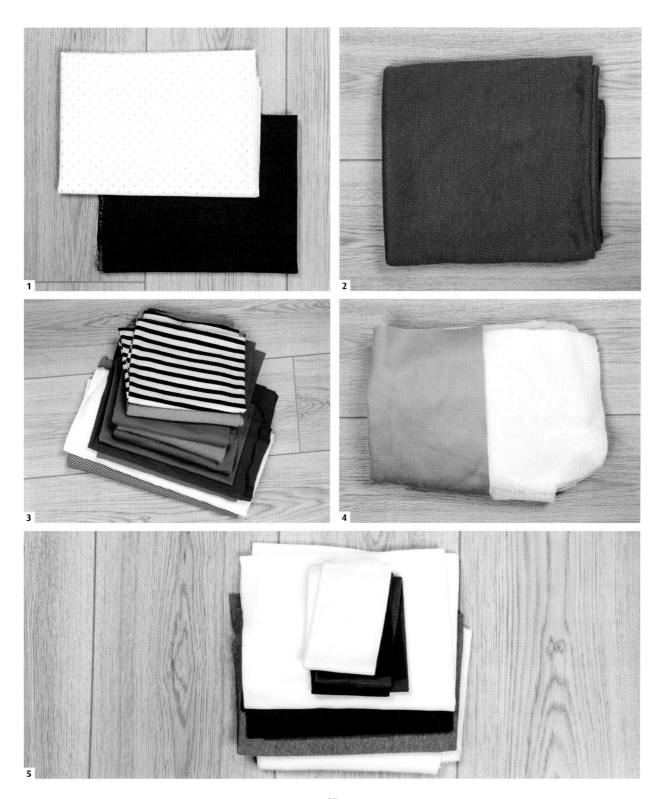

THREAD

On both types of machines, tension is regulated for each individual thread. This gives you great freedom of choice.

REELS OR CONES?
It doesn't matter!

Cones (1)
› Cone threads are finer and smoother. For 4-thread seams, it is often worth reducing the thickness of the seam.
Cones offer a long length of thread which is a good option financially as the overlocker uses lots of thread, particularly in the loopers.

› The problem with cones is storage. If you want to use 4-thread safety stitches (the most common stitch), you will need four cones of an identical colour to match the fabric.
› The best option is to invest in some beige, dark blue and red cones:

- use the beige cones to sew any light-coloured fabrics
- use the dark blue cones to sew any dark-coloured fabrics, including black
- use the red cones to sew any fabrics in the orange/pink/red range. These are the most widely used colours.

› If you are using cones, consider wrapping them in plastic to prevent the thread from unravelling. This allows the threads to unwind properly during sewing.

Reels of thread (2)
› You can use any sort of reel. The advantage of reels is that they can also be used on conventional sewing machines.

Tip: You can always make some 'back-up' reels on the conventional sewing machine.

Worth knowing

In a single seam, threads can be of different thickness, colour and texture.

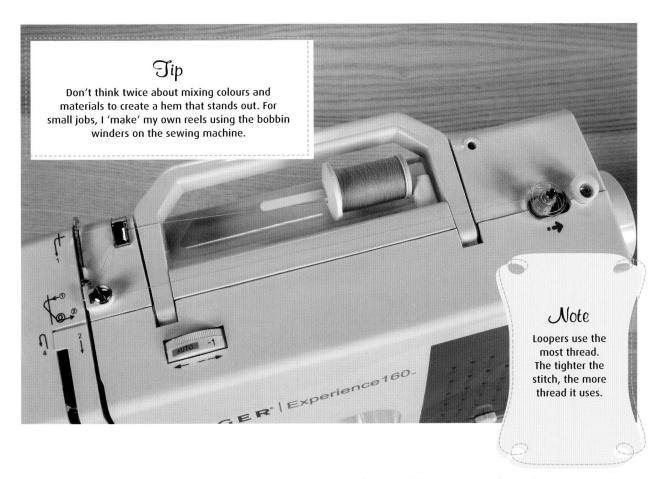

Tip

Don't think twice about mixing colours and materials to create a hem that stands out. For small jobs, I 'make' my own reels using the bobbin winders on the sewing machine.

Note

Loopers use the most thread. The tighter the stitch, the more thread it uses.

TYPES OF THREAD FOR DIFFERENT NEEDLES

› **Cotton or polyester thread** is the most common. (3)

- **Thick threads**, as long as they will go through the eye of the needle, will be useful for solid stitching through thick layers. Use thick needles for this.

Don't forget that you are limited by the size of the eye of the needle! Use a needle-threader for thick threads.

For loopers

› **Transparent thread.** For invisible seams, although they can be a bit scratchy if used for clothes.

› **Woolly nylon thread (4).** Very soft and stretchy. Take care when setting the tension, this type of thread is very stretchy and requires a lower tension than other threads. Woolly nylon is particularly suited to fabric that will be worn next to the skin, for example, T-shirts or baby clothes in soft terry cloth.

› **Silk thread (5).** For decorative hems, flatlock, overlocking sewn on the wrong side so the thread shows, chain stitch embroidery for visible seams and for formal wear.

› **Stretch thread.** Used in the looper for chain stitch on a coverlocker, it allows you to sew gathers at high speed.

› **Embroidery thread (6).** In matt or gloss. Like all silk threads, it is used for stitches that are meant to be seen.

› **Gold and silver threads (7).** The stitching is more irregular, but very stylish. Perfect for visible seams. Sew coverstitch on the coverlocker, place the fabric wrong side out on the machine and sew. Thread from the looper will give your design an attractive finish. However, reels of gold and silver thread don't tend to be very long, so make sure you buy several.

THE MAIN OVERLOCKER STITCHES

The more advanced the machine, the wider the range of stitches it will offer.

For each different stitch you will need to thread the machine differently and use a different needle position. This is what makes these machines seem complicated at first, but keep referring back to the instruction manual where everything is explained.

3-THREAD STRETCH MOCK SAFETY STITCH
Formed with two needles and the lower looper. The upper looper must be blocked using the looper clutch. Used to cut and overlock very fine and/or stretch fabrics.

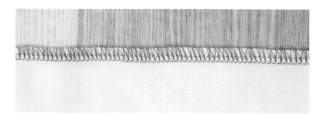

2-THREAD OVERLOCK
Formed with a needle and a looper. Use the clutch button to disengage the second looper. Used to overlock fine or fragile fabrics, such as voile or silk.

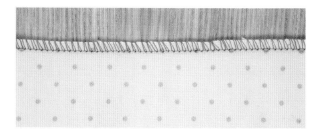

4-THREAD MOCK SAFETY STITCH
Formed with two needles and two loopers. The most commonly used stitch. It can be used to sew and overlock the majority of stretch fabrics. The stitch is neat.

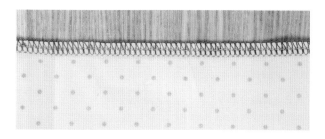

3-THREAD OVERLOCK
Formed with a needle and two loopers. Used to overlock thicker, non-stretch fabrics. This stitch is used for decorative seams, such as flatlock, and sews through the fold of the fabric.

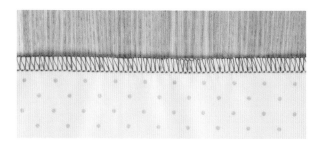

5-THREAD SAFETY STITCH (only for the 5-thread 14 T 968 DC machine)
Sewn using an overlock needle, the middle coverlock needle and three loopers. Used for very thick fabrics, such as denim. Seams are solid and neat.

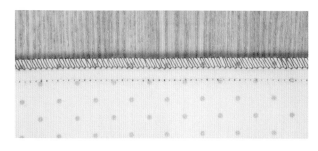

FLATLOCK
Sewn with a 3-thread overlock on folded fabric, with the cutter disabled. This stitch can be decorative.

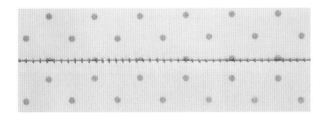

3-THREAD ROLLED HEM (TIGHT)
Stitched with the right needle and two loopers, without the stitch finger (position R). This stitch allows you to hem slightly thicker fabrics. By setting stitch length and width to the minimum you can get a very tight rolled hem. This rolled hem is very attractive on lightweight fabrics.

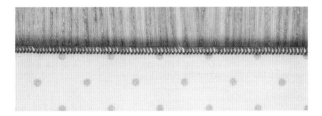

3-THREAD ROLLED HEM (LOOSE)
By setting stitch length to N and the width with the right needle, you will get a looser rolled hem. This rolled hem uses less thread than the tight rolled hem and is more suited to thicker fabric.

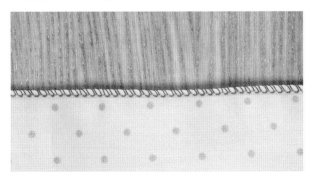

LETTUCE-LEAF EDGE ROLLED HEM
Formed with the right or left needle and two loopers, stitch finger on R, with the differential set at 0.8.

PIN TUCKS
Sewn using the 3-thread overlock, by folding the fabric, deactivating the cutter and sewing along the edge of the fold.

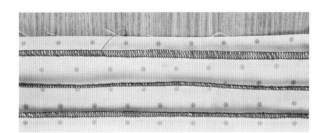

BLIND HEM
Sewn using the 3-thread overlock by folding the fabric and sewing along the edge. Allows you to stitch hems on stretch fabrics very quickly.

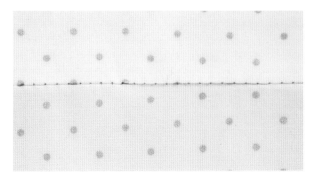

CHAIN STITCH

Sewn using the middle coverlock needle and the looper. This stitch is the only one that can be used in the middle of a piece of fabric. It is used to sew very thick fabrics or to embroider (the embroidery will be on the wrong side of the fabric). The stitch finger must be in position R (rolled hem).

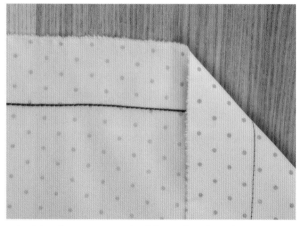

Left of the photo, reverse side of the stitch; right of the photo, right side of the stitch.

3-NEEDLE COVERSTITCH

Position the three needles and the looper thread. Turn the fabric under. Mark the edge of the turn-under on the right side of the fabric. Position the fabric, right side up. Sew along the line you have marked.

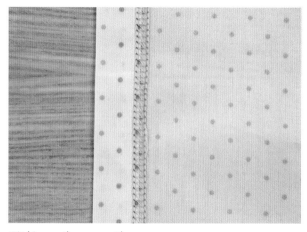

Stitching on the wrong side.

2-NEEDLE COVERSTITCH

For neat, stretchable hems, or a wide hem, position the two needles as far away from each other as possible. For a close coverlock, position the two needles side by side.

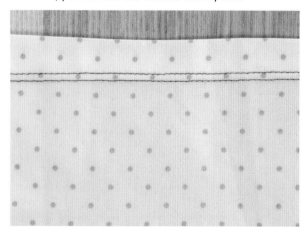

Stitching on the right side.

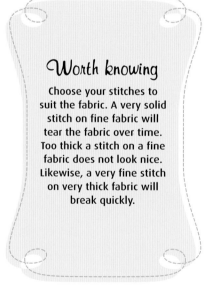

Worth knowing

Choose your stitches to suit the fabric. A very solid stitch on fine fabric will tear the fabric over time. Too thick a stitch on a fine fabric does not look nice. Likewise, a very fine stitch on very thick fabric will break quickly.

UNPICKING AN OVERLOCK
(in this case a 5-thread safety stitch)
1. Using the unpicker, break the needle thread in several places. You can use this method for both overlocking and chain stitch.

2. Pull out the needle thread.
3. The looper thread will come off by itself.

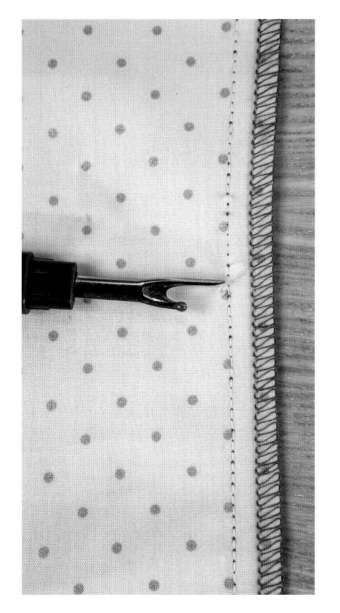

ADJUSTING TENSION ON THE OVERLOCKER THREADS

If the machine is properly adjusted for an overlock, the threads will cross right at the edge. The stitches will be regular, not too loose and the fabric not distorted.

Machine instruction manuals contain tables to help you adjust tension and achieve a good balance. Some machines have a table inside the cover. The 14 T 968 DC machine, also called the Professional 5, has an automatic thread tension adjustment. A useful aid!

ADJUSTING THREAD TENSION

‣ Start by checking the needle threads: is their tension correct?

‣ Check each thread separately. Sew a fairly long chain of stitches around 10cm (4in). This is the length of thread between a tension adjustment dial and the needle. Sew a sample, then check. Repeat for each thread.

A FEW EXAMPLES

‣ The blue needle thread is too loose. There is not enough tension. You need to increase tension.

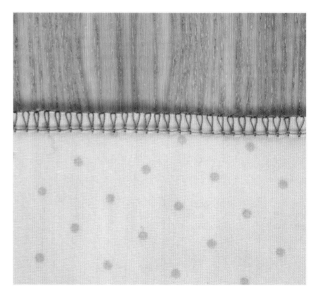

Worth knowing

While this process may seem tricky at first, you will soon learn to recognise the threads and their faults. For this reason, it is worth doing your first seams in different coloured threads, ideally ones that correspond to the colour-coded threading guide.

› The green looper thread is too tight; it is pulling on the lower pink looper thread which, in turn, folds the fabric. You need to decrease tension on the green looper.

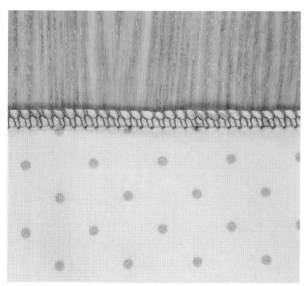

› The pink looper is too tight. It is pulling on the blue thread. Machine instruction manuals give numerous examples for each stitch.

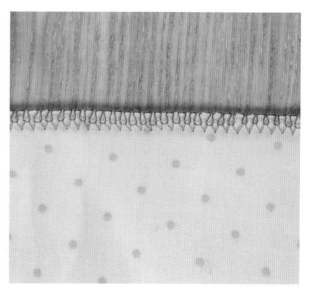

Worth knowing

If the thread tension is not adjusting:

› Make sure you have lowered the presser foot! If the layers are not being held in place by the presser foot, the seam will be uneven: nothing to do with thread tension!
› Threads may have not been fed through the tension discs correctly.
› Threads are not properly engaged.

THREADING THE MACHINE

THREADING

Always follow the threading order. Don't forget that the stitches are formed by threads that are formed into loops.

Instruction manuals will always describe how to thread the machines, and there is generally a guide on the front of the machine itself.

‣ For overlockers:
1. First, the upper looper thread
2. then the lower looper thread
3. the right needle thread
4. the left needle thread
5. and finally, the chain stitch thread (for the combi overlocker/coverlocker).

‣ For coverlockers:
1. First, the furthest right needle
2. then the middle needle thread
3. then the left needle thread
4. and finally the looper.

‣ Only thread the threads required for the stitch: for example, for a 3-thread overlock, thread the upper looper thread, then the lower looper thread, then the right or left needle thread.

‣ To save time, it is tempting to leave all the reels threaded up: this is a mistake! Vibrations may cause the threads to unwind and get tangled with the others. You should remove the reels or cones that you are not using. To stop the cones unwinding, slip an anti-spill net over them.

‣ To thread the different threads, remove the waste bag, open the cover (on some models this will prevent the machine from working) and deactivate the cutter. This will give you space to work.

‣ You can use the threading tweezers to help you get the thread into the right place: some places are difficult to get at without it!

‣ You can thread the loopers and needles with different types of thread. As the tension of the different threads is adjusted individually, you can create all sorts of decorative designs.

‣ Unfortunately, if a thread breaks, you need to rethread all the threads. Often a thread breaks because the machine has not been properly threaded, or a needle is not inserted properly or is blunt. If this is the case, you will often find there is a problem with the other threads as well.

TIE-ON METHOD

See Lesson 8 on page 62.

I do not recommend this method. It looks clever but in reality will not save you any time. When a thread breaks, it won't be of any use. You will need to rethread all the threads in order, including the broken thread.

CLASSIC METHOD

1. Pull the thread guide holder gently upwards and into position.

2. Thread the upper looper first. Place the cone on the relevant thread guide. To ensure the cone unwinds correctly, fit the plastic connector supplied with the machine under the cone. Pass the thread between the tension discs. Follow the green colour-coded thread guide.

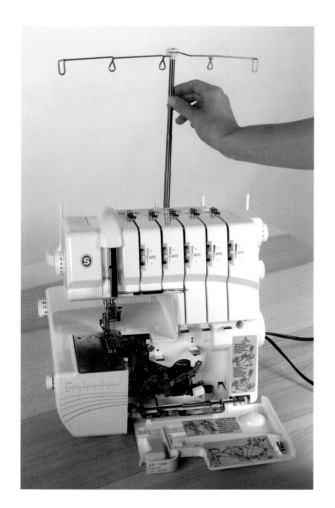

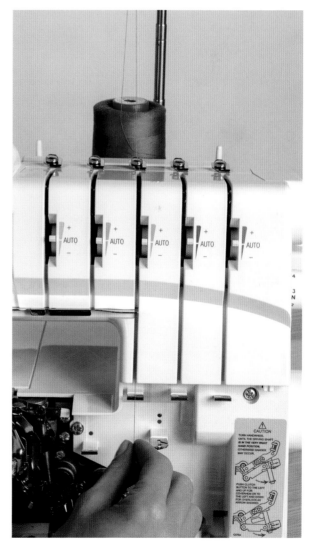

3. Thread the looper using the tweezers.

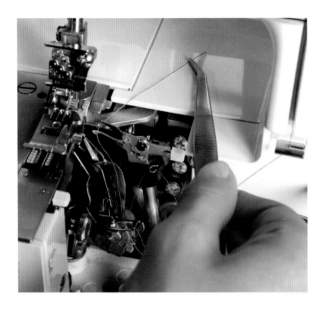

4. Pull a short length of thread towards the back.

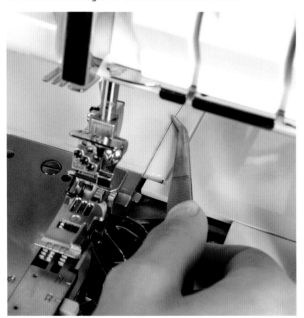

5. Overview of the upper looper thread, colour code: green.

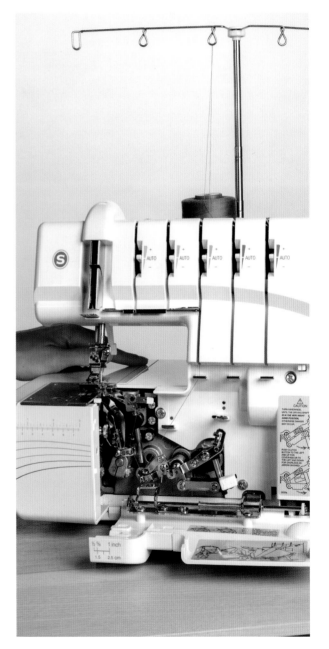

6. Thread the lower looper second. Follow the red colour-coded thread guide. Pass between the tension discs.

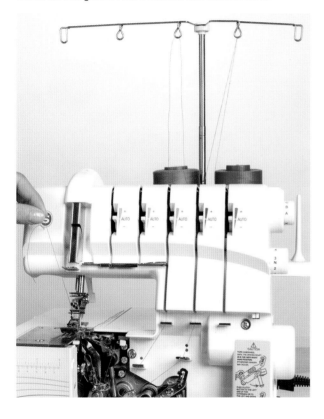

7. Pass the thread through all the thread guides.

8. Raise the red lever and position the thread in the thread guide under the needle plate.

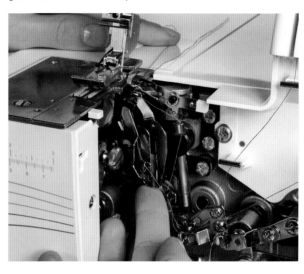

9. Pull the thread towards the back and out.

10. Third, thread the needle thread. Follow the blue colour-coded thread guide. Pass between the tension discs.

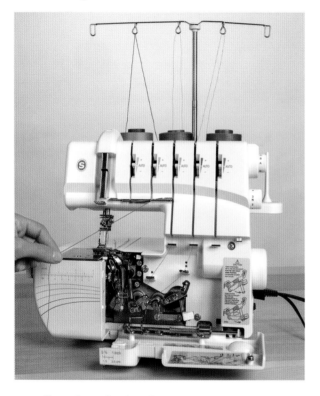

11. Pull gently on the thread.

12. Pass through all the thread guides. This will prevent the threads from getting tangled up.

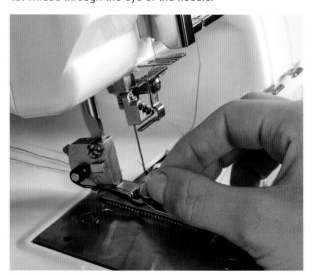

13. Thread through the eye of the needle.

‣ If you are using a second needle, thread this as well. Follow the yellow colour-coded thread guide.

All machines, overlockers and coverlockers are threaded in a similar way.

‣ To check it is correctly threaded, sew a 5cm (2in) chain of stitches and you will see immediately whether everything is properly in place or not.

Chain of rolled hem stitch.

Chain of 3-thread overlock stitches.

Introduction

FIRST USE

▸ Take the machine out of its packaging and place it on a stable table. Make sure you have the instruction manual to hand. Ideally, you should read the manual before getting started. As with any tool, the principle will be the same but functions may differ slightly from one machine to another.

▸ Before plugging in your overlocker, take a look at it. Note the figures on the top dials. The machine has already been set. Don't make any changes to it. Practise lifting the presser foot, opening the cover, handling the cutter and generally getting used to where everything is.

▸ Plug in and sew a few stitches without any fabric. (This is called 'chaining off'). It may surprise you how quickly an overlocker works. It is much faster than a conventional sewing machine. This is a feature you will soon come to appreciate (machines sew and overlock around 1,400 stitches per minute on average).

▸ Feed an offcut of fabric, folded in half, under the pressure foot. Lower the pressure foot. Press on the controller pedal. Look at the stitch. It is formed of loops and stitches. The loops are formed by the threads passing through what are called the loopers and the stitches by the threads passing through the needles. The combination of the number of needle and looper threads creates different stitches. The stitches differ depending on the number of threads used.

▸ The machine comes ready threaded in accordance with the colour code of each thread. The yellow thread follows the yellow thread guide, etc. For first use, I would recommend buying reels of thread that match the colour-coded guides on your overlocker or coverlocker. Colours can differ from model to model. Always thread the new threads in the following order: left (upper) looper, right (lower) looper, right needle then left needle.

▸ Threading seems complicated at first, but by following the guide on the machine you shouldn't find it too hard. You will soon be changing threads or rethreading quickly. See instructions on page 35.

▸ Adjusting the tension of the threads can be another tricky task at first. To get used to it, do some trial runs on different sorts of fabric (still using the coloured threads) such as jersey, cotton, wool or tweed of different thicknesses. If you have kept the colour-coded threads, you will be able to see at a glance which thread is too loose and/or which is too tight. Turn the thread tension dials.

- Where the thread is too tight, the tension is too high. Turn the dial closer to 0.
- Where the thread is too loose, the tension is too low. Turn the dial to a higher number.
- Make a few stitches, then take a look at the seam. You will soon get the tension right.

▸ The instruction manual for each machine will suggest an initial setting for each type of stitch. Refer to the section on the particular stitch and it should give the needle position, the number of loopers and the thread tension.

▸ Only the 5-thread combi overlocker/coverlocker has auto stitch tension adjustment (ATD).

▸ This stage can be tricky at first because it is something you won't have come across with a conventional sewing machine, where tension adjustment for the thread and bobbin is pretty much 'one size fits all'.

▸ For the projects we suggest, in addition to recommended settings, you will be given a few sewing 'tricks' that will help you to achieve full mastery of the machine.

Tip

It might be worth photocopying and laminating the pages about stitches and their tension adjustments. They are useful to have to hand!

GLOSSARY OF TERMS

General sewing terms and practices are the same for the overlocker/coverlocker as for a conventional sewing machine.

‣ Overlock describes the stitching done on the overlocker, whereas on a sewing machine you use the word overstitch. The difference is mainly because the overlocker is a specialist machine that gives a much neater, more finished look.

RIGHT SIDES TOGETHER
This expression is used when sewing together pieces of fabric. The two pieces are placed one on top of the other, right side to right side, with the edge to be stitched lined up. After stitching or overlocking, when you open out the fabric, the stitching is hidden on the wrong side of the fabric.

GRAINS AND BIAS
When cutting out pattern pieces, you need to follow the instructions given on the pattern for bias or grain.

‣ The grain is shown by an arrow on the pattern. It refers to the direction of the fabric's weave. The weave must be parallel to this arrow.

‣ 'Bias' means cut at 45° to the direction of the weave. Bias-cut pieces have more flexibility. If you do not follow these instructions, collars – which should have a certain amount of stretch in them – will not fit properly and clothes that should fall nicely will hang badly.

SEAM ALLOWANCE
None of the patterns in this book, other than the make-up bag, include a seam allowance.

‣ The seam allowance depends on the stitch width, which is defined by the distance between the needle (using the furthest to the right) and the cutter. Add approximately 5mm (¼in) to this, which is cut off by the cutter.

‣ This distance can vary slightly depending on the stitch and the position of the cutter (also known as the stitch-width dial).

‣ The overlocker cuts the fabric, so you need to add a small margin to ensure a neat edge. For this reason, patterns given for overlockers never have seam allowances.

‣ If you buy a pattern that includes a seam allowance and want to change it, just copy the pattern on to paper and add on a seam allowance. Cut out the piece from the fabric. Draw the stitch line on to the fabric using chalk or a marker pen. When stitching, follow the stitching line with the needle. The cutter will cut off the rest. I would strongly recommend tacking/basting the garment by hand or using a conventional sewing machine with very long stitches, so you can try it on, then adjust it to fit as necessary before overlocking. The cutter does not allow any room for error.

‣ You need to take the seam allowance into account for the sides being sewn together, as well as the hem allowance.

‣ Pattern sizes are provided as in the chart below:

WOMEN'S SIZE CHART

SIZES	UK 8/ US 4	UK 10/ US 6	UK 12/ US 8	UK 14/ US 10
BUST	84cm (33in)	88cm (34in)	92cm (36in)	96cm (38in)
WAIST	63cm (25in)	68cm (27in)	73cm (29in)	78cm (31in)
HIPS	88cm (35in)	93cm (37in)	98cm (39in)	103cm (41in)
LENGTH OF OUTSIDE SLEEVE	54cm (21in)	55cm (22in)	55cm (22in)	56 cm (22in)

page 46

page 58

page 66

page 124

page 88

page 98

page 132

page 72

page 80

page 118

page 104

page 110

page 138

page 146

page 154

Project 1

ONE SIZE
SHEET A
SEAM ALLOWANCE INCLUDED
1 PIECE
MACHINES USED: CONVENTIONAL SEWING
MACHINE AND OVERLOCKER

Make-up bag

YOU WILL NEED

- 40cm (15¾in) blue zip
- 30 x 110cm (11¾ x 43¼in) thick cotton fabric
- 3 cones or reels of matching thread
- Standard sewing-box accessories

Worth knowing

This first project is sewn together using a conventional sewing machine. You will use the overlocker to attach the zip and overlock the edges. A simple overlocker will be fine.

INSTRUCTIONS

- Copy the pattern on to paper. This pattern already gives a seam allowance.
- Cut out the outline of the make-up bag twice from the fabric.

OVERLOCKER SETTINGS
- Overlock stitch: 3-thread
- Differential: N (Neutral), because the fabric is non-stretch
- Cutter: activated
- Stitch finger N (Neutral) or S (Overlock) depending on model
- Stitch with 1 single needle – it doesn't matter whether you use the right or left
- Stitch length N
- Thread the 3 threads in the correct order (upper looper, lower looper and then needle), following thread guide
- For non-automatic models, start with a tension of 4-4-4

› Sew a short chain of stitches. Do some test overlock stitches. Adjust thread tension as required. Set ATD A on the automatic model.

› Chain off. When these stitches are even, you know that the machine is properly threaded and you can start overlocking.

Make-up bag

> Overlock each piece of the bag with a 3-thread overlock. You can trim the threads, as they will not be cut the next time you sew.

> Place the zip, right sides together, along the flat edge of the bag. Centre the zip. It should overlap each end by 5cm (2in) (the length of the presser foot).

OVERLOCKER SETTINGS

- Overlock stitch: 3-thread
- Cutter: deactivated, otherwise it might cut the zip
- Stitch finger N (Neutral) or S (Overlock) depending on model
- Use the same threads

Tip
You can overlock using coloured threads that match the fabric of the make-up bags or in a contrasting colour. If this is your first project, it might be best to stick to the colours given on the colour-coded threading guide.

‣ Stitch a sample. Adjust the thread tension as required. Sew a short chain of stitches.

‣ Lower the presser foot. Stitch, ensuring that the layers of fabric are under the presser foot.

‣ Stitch the length of the zip using the 3-thread overlock. Pass the fabric out from under the presser foot to finish the seam.

‣ Match the other flat side of the zip to the other side of the make-up bag opening. Attach using a 3-thread overlock. Trim the threads.

SEWING THE MAKE-UP BAG TOGETHER

‣ Set up the conventional sewing machine.

‣ Half-open the zip (essential for the next step). Place the two parts of the bag one on top of the other, right sides together. Use the sewing machine to stitch right round them, 1cm (½in) from the edge.

‣ Turn the bag the right way out. Oversew by hand at both ends of the zip, adjacent to the side seams. Cut off the ends of the zip with scissors (i.e. kitchen scissors; on no account use sewing scissors as you may damage the blades).

Inserting and removing the needle

1▶ Unscrew ALL the screws.
Note: In the photo, the presser foot has been removed. You can also remove it to give you more space.

2▶ Insert the needle, flat side towards the back.
Use the needle references given for different machines: needles differ from one to the next and stitching will not work if you are using the wrong one.
Tip: If you are inserting several needles, insert them in the same way. If you have removed the presser foot, now is the time to replace it. Turn the knob to lower the needle and check that it does not hit the presser foot.

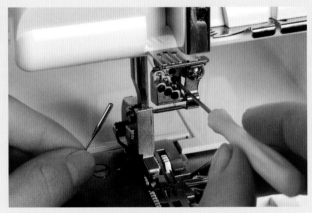

3▶ Hold the needle in place with your finger.
Tip: If you are sewing with a single needle, it is important to remove the second needle; otherwise it will make a line of unsightly small holes and could damage the fabric.

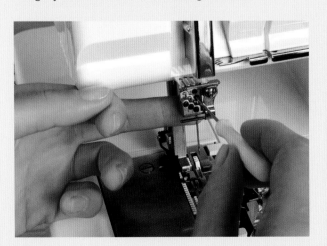

4▶ Tighten all the screws (gently) even if there is no needle so you do not lose the nut.

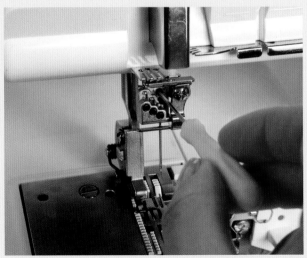

Activating the cutter

1 ▸ Turn the knob upwards to raise the cutter for seams that require trimming (**NB:** some models may have a cutter that you lower rather than raise).

2 ▸ Deactivate the cutter by turning the knob downwards for stitches such as flatlock, or when you do not want to cut the edge of the fabric.

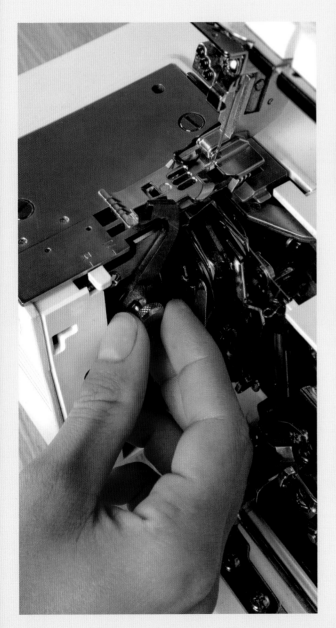

Tip

When you are threading the machine and getting used to handling it, it is best to deactivate the cutter.

Threading : example for the 3-thread overlock

The 3-thread overlock is the stitch most commonly used to overlock thin fabrics, and to overlock and sew together stretch fabrics. Threading is done in exactly the same way whether the overlock is 2-, 3-, 4-, or 5-thread. Thread all the threads in the same order, otherwise the loops will not form correctly:
upper looper, lower looper, right needle, left needle.

1▸ Upper looper
Follow all the green thread guides to thread the upper looper.

2▸ Lower looper
Follow all the pink thread guides to thread the lower looper.

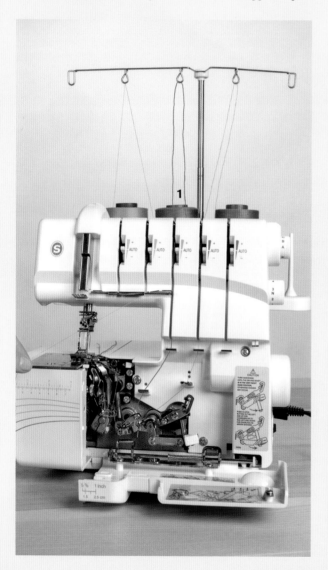

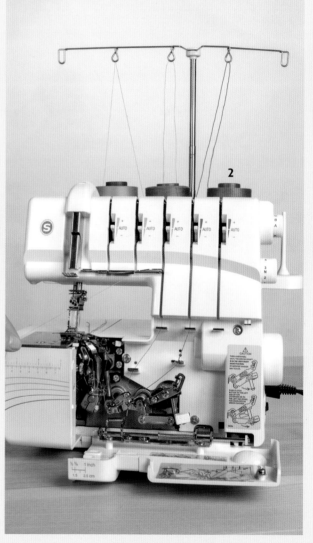

Tip

On some machines a safety device stops you stitching when the cover is open. This is practical because it means you do not have to switch the machine off, so you can still use the light fitted on the machine to help you with the threading.

3 ▸ Right needle
Follow all the blue thread guides to thread the right needle.

4 ▸ Checking key points
Machines come with a threading guide that you should check to ensure the threading is correct. The colour-coded guide is often on the inside of the cover. Each threading point is also marked in the relevant colour.

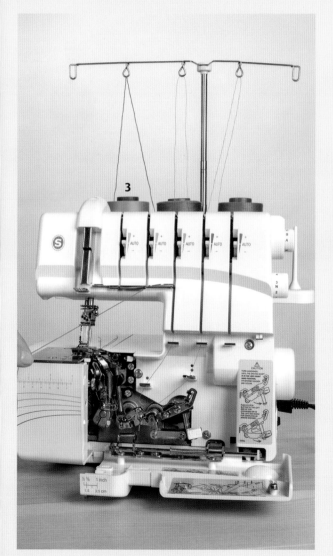

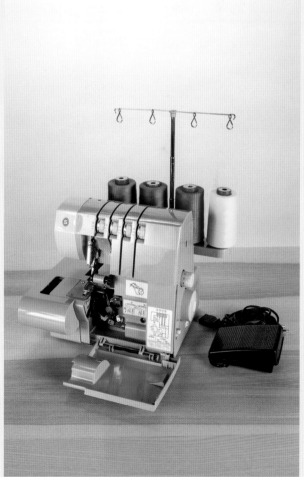

Preparing to overlock

1▸ Draw the seam line using a water-soluble fabric marker pen.

2▸ Activate the cutter by raising it.

3▸ Sew a few stitches without any fabric to 'chain off'. You can see immediately whether or not the stitch is forming well.

4▸ Lift the presser foot.

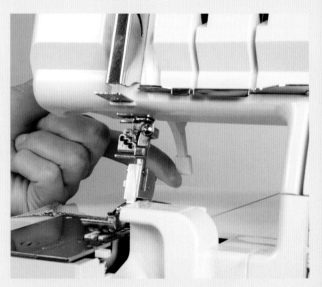

Sewing the first overlock

5▸ Place the fabric in front of the cutter.

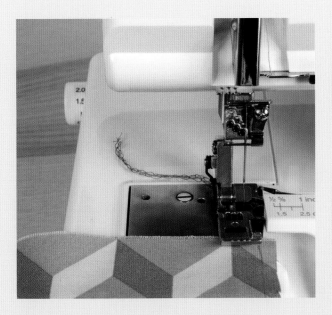

6▸ Start to stitch, following the line you have marked with the pen. The length of fabric trimmed from the edge will fall into the waste bag (in the photo the waste bag has been removed to make it clearer).

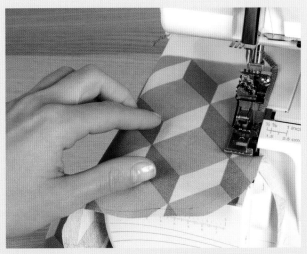

7▸ Continue stitching beyond the fabric to 'chain off'. Then clip the threads.

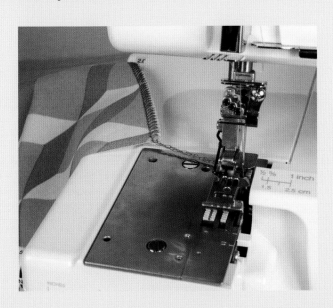

Note

If the chain does not form properly when you run the machine without the fabric, open the cover and check that it is properly threaded. A threading mistake is often evident at a glance. If this is the case, rethread again in the correct order (upper looper, lower looper then needles).

Attaching a zip using the overlocker

1▸ To attach a zip, the zip must be 5cm (2in) longer than the fabric.

2▸ Deactivate the cutter: the zip is not trimmed. Place the zip along one edge of the opening, right sides together, carefully centred. Stitch. Open out the pieces so the right side of the fabric and the zip are face up.

3▸ Place the other side of the bag on the other edge of the zip, right sides together. Check that the two parts of the bag are lined up properly on top of one another. Hold them in place with clips.

4▸ Sew on the second half of the zip. Remove the clips as you go.

Child's comfort blanket

YOU WILL NEED

- 50 x 70cm (19¾ x 27½in) white jersey fabric
- 3 reels of fluorescent pink thread
- 10cm (4in) fancy fluorescent yellow ribbon
- 1 water-soluble fabric marker pen
- 1 darning needle
- 1 gridded fabric-cutting mat
- 1 rotary cutter
- 1 cutting mat
- Standard sewing-box accessories

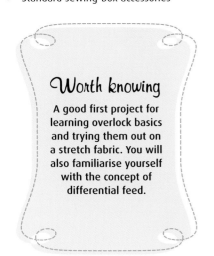

Worth knowing

A good first project for learning overlock basics and trying them out on a stretch fabric. You will also familiarise yourself with the concept of differential feed.

INSTRUCTIONS

‣ Cut a 50 x 70cm (19¾ x 27½in) rectangle in the jersey fabric.
Draw the rectangle using a water-soluble marker pen, then cut approximately 5mm (¼in) round the outside of it. You can now use the line as a guide for your overlocking. The cutter will give the rectangle a clean finish.

OVERLOCKER SETTINGS

- Overlock stitch: 3-thread
- Differential: 1.3 as the fabric is stretchy
- Cutter: activated
- Stitch finger N (Neutral) or S (Overlock) depending on model
- Stitch with 1 single needle – it doesn't matter whether you use the right or left
- Stitch length: N
- Thread the 3 pink threads in the correct order (upper looper, lower looper and then needle), following the machine's threading guide

---

‣ Sew a chain of stitches. Do some sample stitching on a piece of the jersey fabric. Adjust thread tension as required for manual models (ATD A on the automatic model).

‣ Adjusting the differential should not be a problem on this project. However the sewing turns out, even if it is a bit puckered or loose, will not matter with the comfort blanket but it is very good practice!

Child's comfort blanket

- Sew a short chain of stitches.
- Place the fabric in front of the cutter. Lower the presser foot.
- Overlock one side along the marker line.
- Chain off. Overlock the second, then the third side.
- Fold the ribbon in half. Position the ribbon, loop towards the inside, on the edge of the fourth side of the rectangle. Overlock the fourth side. The cutter will neatly trim the jersey and the ends of the ribbon.
- Hide any threads not trimmed by the cutter by weaving them through the hem stitches with a darning needle.

Cutting jersey fabric

1▸ Iron the fabric. Lay the fabric flat on a cutting mat. Place a cutting ruler on top.

2▸ Draw a line in water-soluble marker pen, then cut 5mm (¼in) around this using a rotary cutter. You can cut out the rectangle with sewing scissors but the stretch of the jersey can make this quite tricky.

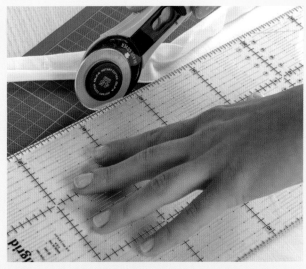

3▸ Remove the ruler without pulling the fabric. Use the ruler to mark the second side at a right angle.

4▸ Cut out the comfort blanket.

Changing threads: tie-on method

1▸ Cut the old threads one by one, leaving a bit hanging.

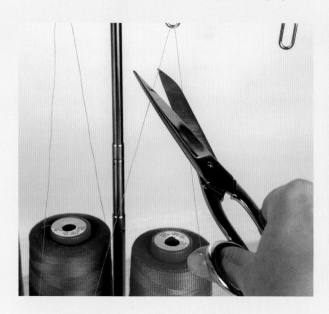

2▸ Replace the old spools of thread with the new ones. Knot the new threads on to the cut threads.

3▸ Make a note of the tension settings, then adjust to achieve a very loose tension (this helps the knotted thread to pass more easily through the tension dials).

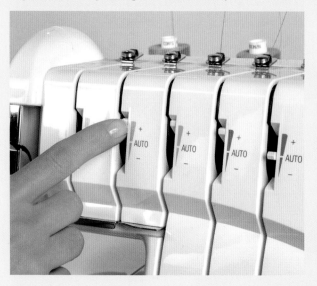

4▸ Pull gently on each looper thread until the knot has passed through all looper guides. With the needle threads, when the knot reaches the needle, cut it off. Thread the new thread through the needle. Reset to the tensions you noted previously.

Adjusting the thread tension

1▶ Sew a chain of stitches, then use some scrap fabric to sew a test hem.

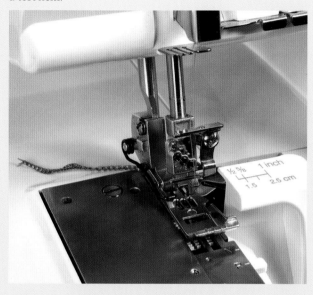

2▶ Check the sewing for the following:

2a. The pink thread looks very loose and baggy. The pink thread comes from the lower looper (look at the colour coding on the machine). To achieve an attractive stitch, you need to increase the tension on the pink thread.

2b. The green thread looks very loose. Increase the green thread tension.

2c. The green thread (lower looper) is pulling too much on the pink thread. Decrease the green thread tension.

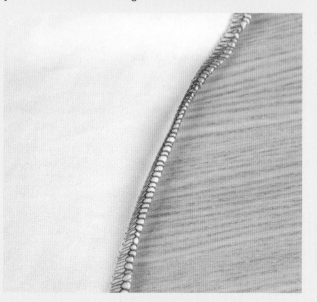

3▶ Refer to the machine manual. All machine instruction manuals have tables giving recommended thread tensions for each stitch type, depending on the thickness of the fabric you are using. These are a good starting point. Do some sample stitches then start the hem when you think the tension is right. A sign of good tension is when the threads cross at the very edge.

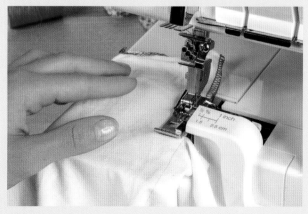

Stitching a right-angle corner

1▸ Draw the rectangle to be overlocked in water-soluble marker pen (it is difficult to stitch in a straight line without a guide line marked on the fabric). Overlock the first side. There is no need to cut off the initial and final stitch chains as the cutter will do this.

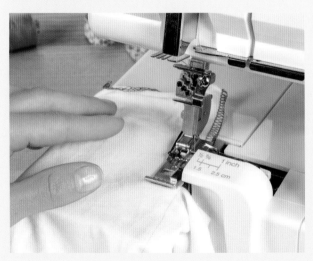

2▸ Overlock the second side following the guide line. The cutter will cut the stitch chain of the previous overlock.

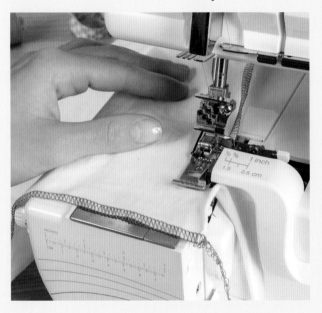

3▸ Line up the ends of the ribbon loop with the edge of the fourth side. Hold in place with a clip.

4▸ Overlock the third and fourth side. The loop is sewn on by the overlocking. Remove the clip before it gets to the cutter.

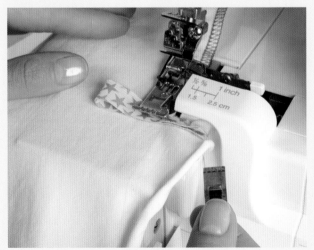

Securing the ends of threads with a darning needle or thread glue

1▶ Overlock the four sides. The stitch chain from the last side will be long because it hasn't been cut off yet. Thread it through a darning needle.

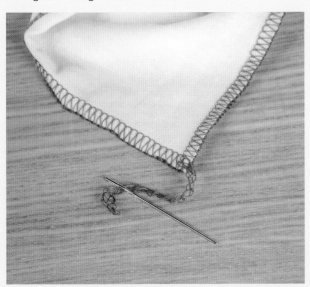

2▶ Weave the stitch chain into the overlock stitches using the darning needle.

3▶ You can also trim the threads close to the end of the overlock hem.

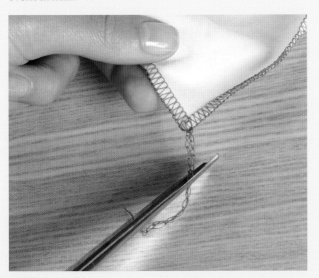

4▶ Stick the thread ends into place with fabric glue. This method should not be used on projects that will be washed frequently as water-based fabric glue will eventually dissolve.

Project 3

NO PATTERN
MACHINE USED: OVERLOCKER

Headbands

YOU WILL NEED

- › 30 x 60cm (11¾ x 23¾in) jersey fabric
- › 3 reels or cones of matching thread
- › 60cm (23¾in) floral print rattail cord
- › Standard sewing-box accessories

Worth knowing

Headbands are fun to make and a very good exercise in adjusting stitch tension. As each fabric is different, hemming them is a good way to get used to the machine.

INSTRUCTIONS

› Cut 5 x 60cm (2 x 23¾in) rectangles from the jersey fabric.

OVERLOCKER SETTINGS
- Overlock stitch: 3 threads
- Differential: 1.3 to 1.5 because the fabric is stretchy
- Cutter: activated
- Stitch finger N (Neutral) or S (Overlock) depending on model
- Sew with the right needle
- Stitch length N
- Thread the 3 threads in the correct order (upper looper, lower looper and right needle), in accordance with the machine's threading guide
- Decrease stitch width to the minimum, to prevent the fabric being too thick

› Stitch a sample. Adjust the thread tension as required (ATD A on the automatic model).

› Sew a short chain of stitches.

› Fold the jersey rectangles in half lengthways, right sides together, to form a tube, then stitch along the long edge using a 3-thread overlock.

› Use a safety pin to turn the headband the right way out (see page 71).

Headbands

‣ Try the headband on (or on the person who is going to wear it). Cut to the right length if necessary.

‣ Stitch the two short ends of the headband together using a 3-thread overlock.

VARIATIONS

Floral print headband (shown on page 67)
‣ Cut some narrower rectangles and make bands as above. Place the bands next to the floral print cord. Using big stitches, sew the ends of the bands together by hand.

Knotted headband
‣ Cut a rectangle to form a band that is longer than the circumference of your head, then make the headband following the steps above. Turn the ends in. Overlock the ends by hand. Tie the headband round your head with a bow.

Stitch widths

There are several ways of making stitches wider or narrower.

1▶ Stitch with the left needle: the stitch will be wider as you are using the maximum distance between cutter and needle.

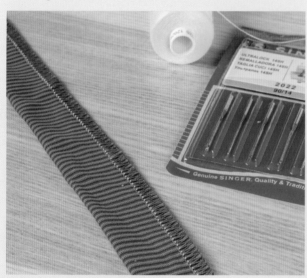

2▶ For a narrower stitch, sew with the right needle (this decreases the distance between the cutter and the needle).

3▶ Compare the two widths.

Worth knowing

Some machines have a 'stitch width' knob. As you turn the knob, you change the stitch width by moving the needle block nearer or further away. The stitch width is important in cutting garments because you need to add a seam allowance (see page 77).

Adjusting the differential feed

There are two sets of feed dogs under the presser foot, which act as fabric guides. It is possible to adjust the feed, which is often referred to as the 'differential'.

1 ▶ Set at 1, the differential is said to be 'Neutral'. This setting is for non-stretch fabrics that do not get pulled out of shape.

2 ▶ Set at more than 1, the differential is used for stretch fabrics and will prevent any puckering created by the presser foot.

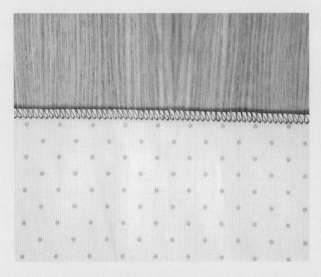

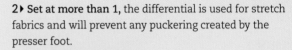

3 ▶ Set at less than 1, the differential will stretch the fabric, creating a wavy edge.

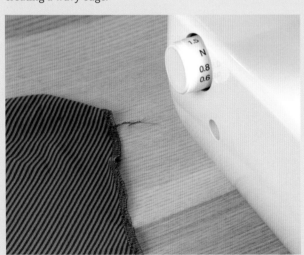

Worth knowing
The stretch in jersey fabric is not the same in all directions.

Turning a band inside out

1▸ Sew a tube by folding a strip of fabric in half lengthways. Push a safety pin through the end of the tube.

2▸ Close the safety pin and slip it into the end of the tube.

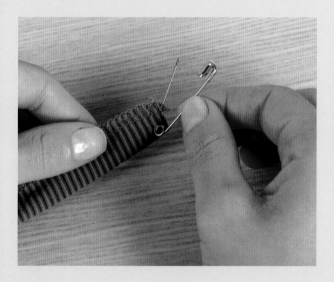

3▸ Push the safety pin through the inside of the tube to the other end.

4▸ Turn the tube inside out by pulling the safety pin out of the other end.

SIZES: FROM 8 TO 14 (US 4 TO 10)
SHEET B
SEAM ALLOWANCE NOT INCLUDED
2 PIECES
MACHINE USED: OVERLOCKER

My first T-shirts

YOU WILL NEED

- 70 x 140cm (27½ x 55in) pink jersey
- 70 x 140cm (27½ x 55in) purple jersey
- 3 reels or cones of matching thread
- 10cm (4in) of seam binding for the shoulders
- Standard sewing-box accessories

Worth knowing

You will soon be a fan of these quick-sew T-shirts. Use whichever finish you prefer: a tight-rolled hem or unhemmed edge.

INSTRUCTIONS

‣ The T-shirts will be sewn together using a 3-thread safety stitch. Sew a stitch sample. Measure the stitch width.

‣ Copy the pattern adding a seam allowance (width of stitch plus about 5mm/¼in) along the sides and shoulders only. The neck, armholes and bottom edge do not have a seam or hem, so cut in accordance with the pattern.

‣ Cut a front and back from the fabric, ensuring the grain of the fabric is in the right direction.

OVERLOCKER SETTINGS
- Overlock stitch: 3-thread
- Differential: 1.3 as the fabric is stretchy
- Cutter: activated
- Stitch finger N (Neutral) or S (Overlock) depending on model
- Stitch with a single needle – it doesn't matter whether you use the right or left
- Stitch length: N
- Thread the three threads in the correct order (upper looper, lower loop, needle)

‣ Sew a stitch sample. Adjust the thread tension as required (tension A on the automatic model).

‣ Sew a short chain of stitches.

‣ Feed the seam binding into the presser foot.

‣ Place the front on the back, right sides together. Line up the shoulders. Stitch the shoulders together, taking the seam binding into the seam. Stitch one shoulder then the other as if they were the same seam.

‣ Cut the stitching and the seam binding between the two shoulders.

PREPARING THE ROLLED HEMS ROUND THE NECK AND ARMHOLES

OVERLOCKER SETTINGS

- Stitch: 3-thread rolled hem
- Differential: 2
- Cutter: activated
- Stitch finger: R for rolled
- Stitch with a single needle: the right needle for a rolled hem
- Reduce stitch length to 1
- Thread the three threads in the correct order (upper looper and lower looper, needle)

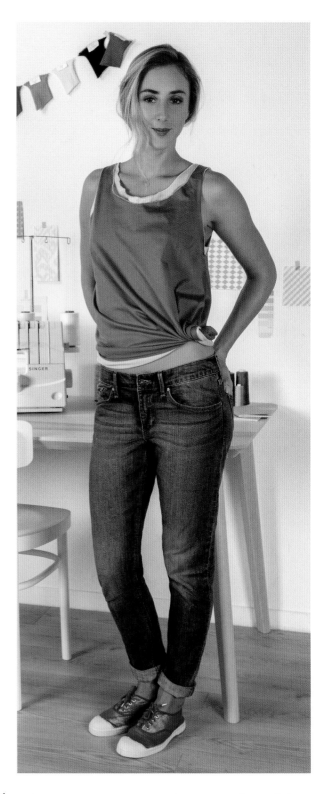

‣ Stitch a sample. Adjust thread tension as required (ATD C on the automatic model). Reduce stitch width with the cutter knob.

‣ Sew a short chain of stitches.

‣ Stitch round the neckline, right side up. Start and finish the stitching on one shoulder. Take care with the last 2.5cm (1in) of the stitching, withdrawing the cutter, otherwise the cutter will trim off the start of the rolled hem.

‣ Finish by hiding any untrimmed threads by weaving them through the stitching.

‣ Stitch round the armholes using rolled hem stitching. As the sides of the T-shirt have not yet been sewn up, the rolled hem will be easier to do.

SET OVERLOCKER TO A 3-THREAD SAFETY STITCH

‣ Sew the sides of the T-shirt, right sides together. Hide thread ends by weaving them through the overlock.

‣ Cut neatly along the bottom of the T-shirt; there is no hem on these T-shirts. You could do a rolled hem around the neckline and armholes – this is a speedy way of making T-shirts.

Tip
You can sew the rolled hem in a contrasting colour for an individually stylish look.

Measuring stitch width

The patterns do not include seam allowance. Machines have different stitch widths. You can also vary the width using the positioning knob (which moves the cutter) or by changing needle position. You need to sew some sample stitches with the stitch that you are going to use before you copy the pattern.

1▶ Do some test stitches, then measure the stitch width.

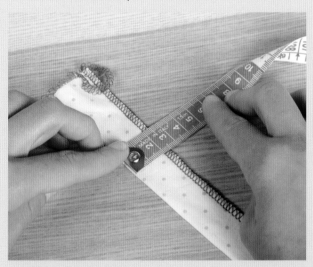

2▶ Pin the pattern to the fabric.

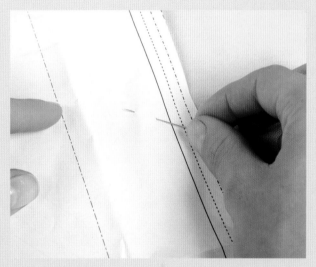

3▶ Add on the value of the stitch width plus a 3mm (¹/₈in) allowance which will be the amount trimmed by the cutter.

4▶ Cut out the fabric.
Tip: To avoid recalculating the allowance each time, it is worth making a little card as a reference guide with the stitches and their settings, plus seam allowance values.

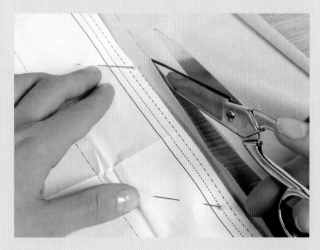

Adding seam binding

To prevent certain seams pulling out of shape, add seam binding during stitching.
This lesson shows seam binding the shoulders.

1▸ Pass the binding into the presser foot aperture. The seam binding that goes through the presser foot will not be cut by the cutter.

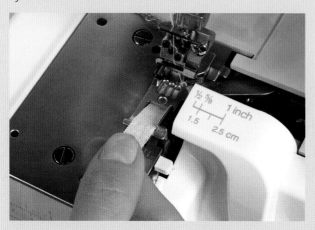

2▸ Sew a short chain of stitches and feed in the binding.

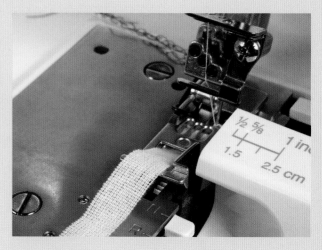

3▸ Position the layers of fabric under the presser foot. **Note:** the seam binding will be longer than the width of the shoulder and will be trimmed later.

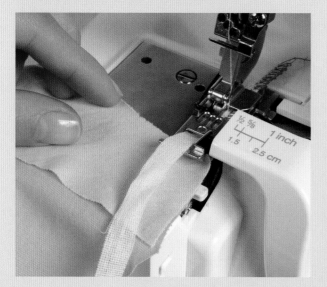

4▸ Stitch the two shoulders in one go. Then cut the binding between the two shoulders to separate them.

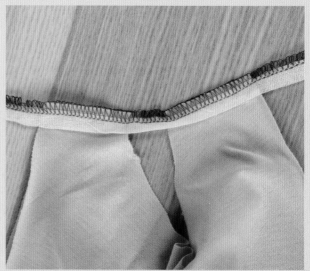

Sewing a rolled hem

Rolled hems make an attractive finish and allow you to sew a very narrow hem.

1▸ Rolled hems are stitched on the right side of the fabric. They require special settings on the overlocker: right needle for a tight stitch, the minimum stitch width and length, stitch finger at R, cutter activated for a neat finish, one needle thread and two loopers. Set an automatic machine to C.

3▸ Feed the fabric under the presser foot.

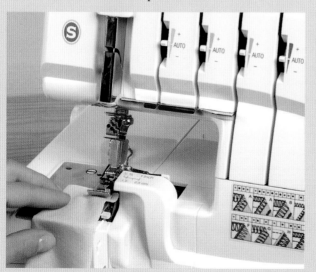

2▸ Sew a chain of stitches.

4▸ Stitch right along the edge. If you are sewing a rolled hem in the round, deactivate the cutter for the last 4cm (1½in).
Tip: Always concentrate on the cutter and the stitch. Your left hand should support the presser foot and help guide the fabric through – do not pull on it.

SIZES: FROM 8 TO 14 (US 4 TO 10)
SHEET A
SEAM ALLOWANCE NOT INCLUDED
3 PIECES
MACHINES USED: OVERLOCKER AND COVERLOCKER

Raglan T-shirt

YOU WILL NEED

- 100 x 140cm (39½ x 55in) pink jersey
- 4 reels or cones of red thread
- 80cm (31½in) of silver-edged pink elastic
- Standard sewing-box accessories

Tip

This raglan T-shirt looks very stylish with contrasting hems. The silver-edged elastic means the neckline doesn't droop.

INSTRUCTIONS

› The T-shirt will be sewn using a 4-thread mock safety stitch. Sew a stitch sample and measure the stitch width. Copy the pattern adding a seam allowance (stitch width plus approximately 5mm/¼in) along the sides of the front and back and the sides of the sleeves. Do not add a seam allowance to the neckline or to the end of the sleeves. Add 3cm (1¼in) to the bottom for the hem.

› Cut a front, back and two sleeves from the fabric, ensuring the grain of the fabric runs in the right direction.

OVERLOCKER SETTINGS

- Overlock: 4-stitch mock safety stitch
- Differential: 1.5 as the fabric is stretchy
- Cutter: activated
- Stitch finger N (Neutral) or S (Overlock) depending on the model
- Stitch with two needles, right and left
- Stitch length: N
- Thread the four threads in the correct order (upper looper and lower looper, then right needle, then left needle)

› Sew a short chain of stitches.

› Sew a sample. Adjust thread tension as required for manual models (ATD A on the automatic model).

› Sew a short chain of stitches.

PREPARING THE SLEEVES

Turn up the bottom of the sleeve by 2cm (¾in) twice (right sides together). Tack/baste with big stitches to hold the turn-up in place.

‣ Line up the front of the sleeve with the front of the T-shirt. Hold in place with small clips. Sew together using a 4-thread mock safety stitch.

‣ Line up the back of the sleeve with the back of the T-shirt. Sew together using a 4-thread mock safety stitch. If you are a beginner, you might prefer to tack/baste them first. However, YOU MUST NOT USE PINS!

‣ Attach the second sleeve in the same way.

‣ The turn-ups on the sleeves will be taken into the seams – hold the turn-ups in place in the middle with a small hand stitch. Hide any untrimmed threads by weaving through the stitching using a darning needle.

SEWING THE T-SHIRT TOGETHER

Place front on back, right sides together. Sew the sides using a 4-thread mock safety overlock.

ASSEMBLING THE NECK

OVERLOCKER SETTINGS

- Stitch: 3-thread overlock
- Differential: 2 (otherwise the T-shirt will be very low-necked)
- Cutter: deactivated to make sure it doesn't cut the elastic
- Right needle for a narrow stitch width
- Stitch finger: N or S (depending on model)
- Stitch length: position N
- Thread the 3 threads in the correct order (upper looper and lower looper, then right needle)

› Mark the halves and the quarters on the elastic with small clips. Mark the halfway and quarterway sections of the neckline with small clips. Place the elastic on the neckline, right sides together, silver edge downwards. Make sure that the clips marking the halfway and quarterway sections are aligned. Hold in place with small clips. Beginners might want to tack/baste into place to ensure the elastic is evenly distributed.

› Chain off.

› Sew on the elastic using a 3-thread overlock. Fold the elastic over to the inside of the T-shirt to make the silver edge stand out on the right side.

COVERLOCKER SETTINGS

- Chain stitch
- Thread the middle needle for an attractive stitch
- Thread the looper

› Sew round the neckline in chain stitch.

SEWING THE BOTTOM HEM

Fold a hem all round the bottom as in Lesson 23, page 94. Iron to mark the fold.

OVERLOCKER SETTINGS

- Overlock stitch: 3 narrow threads
- Differential: 1.5 as the fabric is stretchy
- Cutter: activated
- Stitch finger: N or S (depending on model)
- Sew with the right needle
- Stitch length 4 (very long)
- Thread the 3 threads in the correct order (upper looper and lower looper, then right needle)

› Fit the blind hem presser foot.

› Sew a short chain of stitches. Adjust the thread tension as required (ATD A on the automatic model).

› Position the folded fabric along the guide. Stitch.

Note
The sleeves are not hemmed because the edge is hidden by the double turn-up.

Sewing on raglan sleeves

1▸ After you have cut out the front, the back and the sleeves, line up the front of the sleeve with the front of the armhole on the body of the T-shirt, right sides together. Stitch together.

2▸ To create a roll-up, fold up the bottom of the sleeve twice (right sides together) and sew with the overlocker.

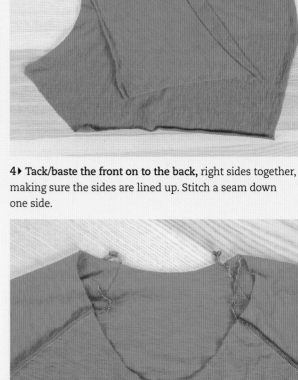

3▸ Line up the back of the sleeve with the armhole of the back of the T-shirt, right sides together. Hold in place with small clips, then stitch together.

4▸ Tack/baste the front on to the back, right sides together, making sure the sides are lined up. Stitch a seam down one side.

Attaching an elastic neck

1▸ Hide the ends of the threads used to sew the T-shirt together by weaving them through the hem stitches as they will not be cut off by the cutter on the next seam.

2▸ Sew the elastic into a circle. The elastic will prevent the neckline from drooping. Mark the halfway and quarterway points of the neckline using little clips. Fold in half and attach a clip.

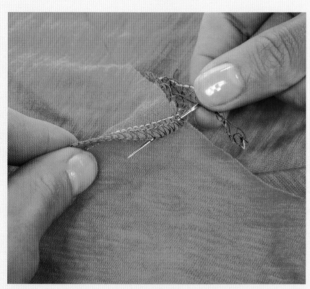

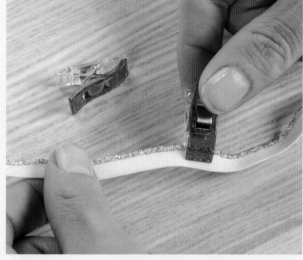

3▸ Mark the halfway and quarterway points round the neckline with clips.

4▸ Place the elastic round the neckline, right sides together. Line up the halfway and quarterway markers. Beginners may want to tack/baste the elastic into place, then sew using a 3-thread overlock, without the cutter.

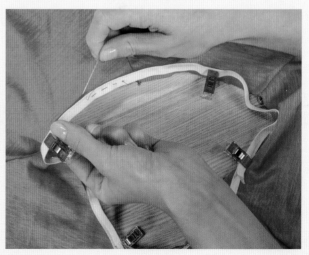

Finishing the neck with chain stitch

1▸ Sew on the elastic using a 3-thread overlock, right sides together, with the silver edge towards the bottom of the T-shirt.

2▸ Fold the elastic over against the wrong side of the T-shirt; the contrast colour will be visible on the right side.

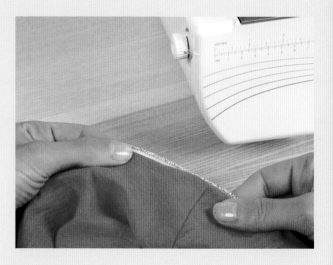

3▸ Change the setting of the machine if you are using a 5-thread machine, or change to the coverlocker. Set to chain stitch. It is important to use the middle needle to obtain an attractive loop with 1 looper thread.
Note: If you are not using a looper on the 5-thread model, remember to use the clutch button to disengage the second looper.
Adjust the differential feed: it should be greater than 1, around 1.5 to 2 to absorb the stretch). Sew without the cutter on the right side of the fabric.

4▸ To ensure the hem is neat, pull gently on the fabric and the elastic.

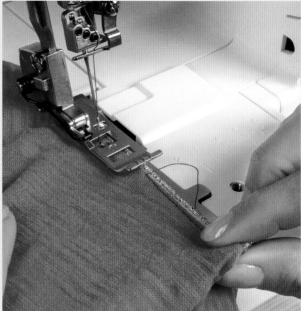

Stitching a blind hem

1▶ Turn up the bottom of the T-shirt towards the wrong side of the fabric by about 2cm (¾in). Iron in the crease of the fold.

2▶ Fold the bottom of the T-shirt back to the right side. Leave approximately 5mm (¼in) overhanging the first fold. Iron to mark the crease.

3▶ Adjust the settings of the machine. Change to a 3-thread overlock, increase the stitch length to maximum and activate the cutter. Swap to the special blind hem presser foot. This has a guide on the right.

4▶ Chain off. Insert the folded edge under the presser foot. Line up the fold with the right-hand guide of the presser foot. The stitch will form the hem, while the cutter will neatly trim off the edge of the fabric. Sew to ensure that the needle just runs along the edge of the fabric.

SIZES: FROM 8 TO 14 (US 4 TO 10)
SHEET A
SEAM AND HEM ALLOWANCE NOT INCLUDED
2 PIECES
MACHINES USED: OVERLOCKER AND COVERLOCKER

Embroidered top

YOU WILL NEED

- 50 x 140cm (19¾ x 55in) thick jersey fabric without too much stretch
- 4 reels or cones of matching thread
- 2 reels of silk thread (or gloss thread) for each chain stitch colour
- Standard sewing-box accessories

INSTRUCTIONS

‣ The top is sewn using a 4-thread safety stitch. Sew a sample. Measure stitch width. Copy the pattern adding a seam allowance (width of stitch plus about 5mm/¼in). Only the sides have a seam. Add 2.5cm (1in) hem seam allowance at the top and the bottom of the top.

‣ Cut the front and back from the fabric.

COVERLOCKER SETTINGS

- Chain stitch
- Thread the middle needle with silk thread (to make an attractive stitch)
- Thread the looper with silk thread in the same colour

Worth knowing

This top is very quick to sew and is good practice for chain stitch embroidery. Choose a thick jersey fabric. Don't hesitate to fit the top if it is too wide. It is meant to be tight. If you make it shorter, it can be worn under a very low-cut top. If you make it longer, you will be the belle of the ball in your little dress!

Embroidered top

- On the wrong side of the top, use a water-soluble fabric marker to mark the curved lines that will be the stems.

- On the wrong side of the fabric, sew along the guide lines that you marked. The chain stitch will then be visible on the right side.

- Change the colours of the threads. When you are comfortable with the technique, turn over the fabric and draw on some leaves at the base of the stems.

- If you want, add more stems and leaves.

- Knot then weave in the ends of the threads.

OVERLOCKER SETTINGS

- Overlock: 4-stitch mock safety
- Differential: 1.3 as the fabric is stretchy
- Cutter: activated
- Stitch finger N (Neutral) or S (Overlock) depending on model
- Stitch with 2 needles, right and left
- Stitch length N
- Thread the 4 threads in the correct order (upper looper and lower looper, then right needle, then left needle)

‣ Chain off. Stitch a sample. Adjust the thread tension as required for manual models (ATD A on the automatic model).

‣ Chain off a few stitches.

‣ Place the front on the back, right sides together. Sew the sides together using a 4-thread mock safety stitch.

STITCHING THE TOP AND BOTTOM HEMS

COVERLOCKER SETTINGS
- Wide coverstitch
- If you have combi overlocker/coverlocker, set it
  to the coverlocker setting (see Lesson 32, page 116)
- Differential: 1.3
- Install the right and left needles
- Thread the looper and the two needles

‣ Turn in a 2.5cm (1in) hem to the wrong side, all round the top edge. Iron in the fold. Ironing it will make a slight mark on the right side of the fabric to give you a stitch line.

‣ Place the top edge of the wrong side on the machine, so right side up. You can no longer see the fold.

‣ Stitch right round. Stop stitching as soon as you get back to the beginning so you don't sew over the previous stitches. Tie a knot on the wrong side.

Chain stitch embroidery using the coverlocker

1▶ Adjust the coverlocker to chain stitch: thread the single looper with coloured thread, which can be wool, cotton or silk. Note that there is no cutter on a coverlocker; the stitches can be done in the middle of a piece of fabric.

2▶ Thread the middle needle for an attractive stitch.

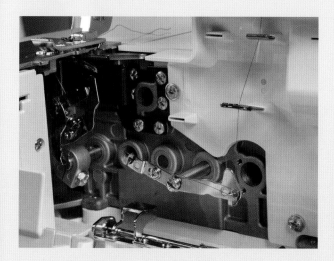

3▶ Draw your design on the wrong side of the fabric using a textile pen or tailor's chalk.

4▶ Stitch curved lines to make the stalks and leaves. The chain stitch will be visible on the other side of the fabric.

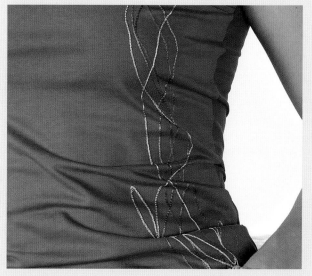

Preparing a hem on the coverlocker

1▶ Fold in 2–3cm (¾–1¼in) to the wrong side. Iron in the fold.

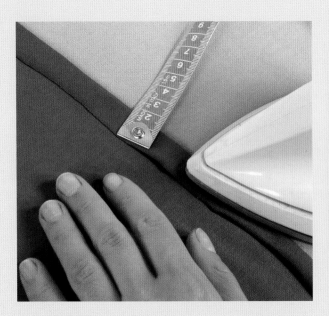

2▶ The turn-up will not be visible while you are sewing. It will help if you crease the fold with your finger, then go over it with a water-soluble marker pen on the right side (when you are used to it you can skip this stage).

3▶ Feed the fabric under the presser foot. Lower the presser foot. Centre the line between the needles. Note that when you are using the coverlocker, you do not begin a seam by chaining off. There is only one looper so the stitch is much easier to adjust.

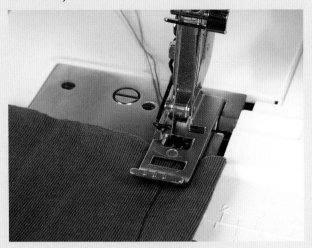

4▶ Sew along the marked line.

Finishing a coverstitch hem in the round

1▸ Sew the hem following the guide line. When finishing a hem, sew the last stitches manually by turning the wheel without pressing on the pedal so the stitches end precisely where they began.

2▸ To release the fabric without tearing, pull on the first needle thread to release it, then cut it.

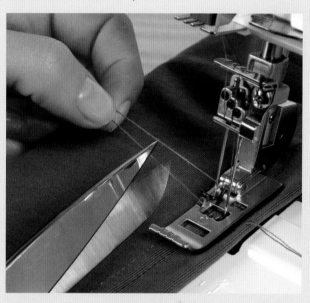

3▸ Pull on the thread in the second needle, then cut.

4▸ Lift the presser foot, pull gently on the fabric and cut the looper thread.

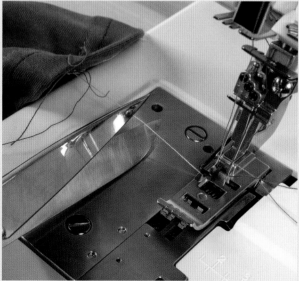

Tying a knot in coverstitch

1▸ Keep the threads long. Separate the threads.

2▸ Knot a needle thread to the looper thread.

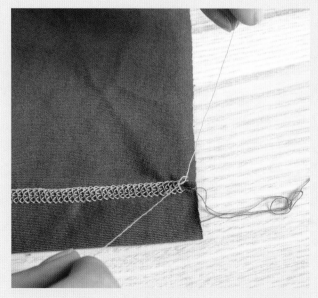

3▸ Knot the second needle thread to the third needle thread if there is one. Otherwise knot the needle thread with the looper thread.

4▸ Clip the threads.

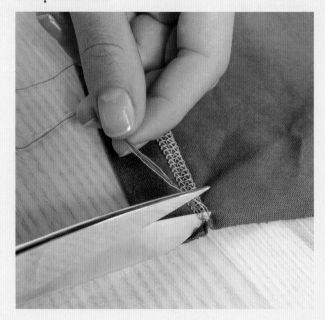

Unpicking a coverstitched seam

1 ▸ Using an unpicker (not scissors as they will damage the fabric), cut through a needle thread.

2 ▸ Still using the unpicker, pull on the needle thread to unpick it a little.

3 ▸ Cut the other needle threads. Unpick a small section.

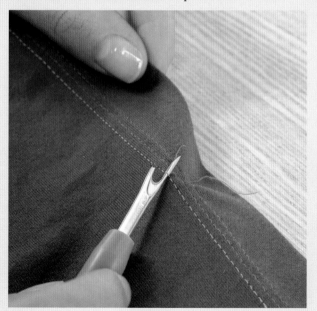

4 ▸ The looper thread on the other side is no longer held in place and will unravel itself.

SIZES: FROM 8 TO 14 (US 4 TO 10)
SHEET B
SEAM ALLOWANCE NOT INCLUDED
3 PIECES
MACHINES USED: CONVENTIONAL SEWING MACHINE,
OVERLOCKER, COVERLOCKER

Sailor–stripe top

YOU WILL NEED

- 150 x 140cm (59 x 55in) thick, sailor-stripe jersey fabric
- 40cm (15¾in) of 3cm (1¼in) wide fluorescent yellow bias binding to reinforce the neck and sleeve hems
- 30cm (11¾in) of white seam binding for the shoulders
- 3 reels or cones of fluorescent yellow thread
- 4 reels or cones of white thread

Worth knowing

This fashionable, longer, figure-hugging take on a traditional sailor top, with fluorescent yellow threads, is good training in coverstitching necks and hems.

INSTRUCTIONS

- The top is sewn using a 4-thread mock safety stitch.
Sew a stitch sample. Measure the stitch width. Copy the pattern adding a seam allowance (stitch width plus about 5mm/¼in) to all parts, except the front neckline, the bottom of the sleeves, and the bottom of the front and back.

- Add a 2cm (¾in) hem allowance to the front neckline, the bottom of the sleeves, and the bottom of the front and back.

- Cut a front, back and two sleeves from the fabric, ensuring the grain of the fabric runs in the right direction.
Make sure you position the pattern so that the stripes of the sleeves all align. To do this you need to fold the fabric in two and precisely match the stripes. You may also want the stripes on the sleeves to align with those on the body.

- Pin at regular intervals to make sure the stripes line up. Decide where you want the white band to be. Cut.

OVERLOCKER SETTINGS

- Overlock: 4-thread mock safety
- Differential: 1.3 as the fabric is stretchy
- Cutter: activated
- Stitch finger: N (Neutral) or S (Overlock) depending on model
- Stitch with 2 needles, right and left
- Stitch length N
- Thread 4 white threads, following the threading order (upper looper and lower looper, then right needle and left needle)

Sailor-stripe top

- Sew a stitch chain. Sew a sample seam. Adjust thread tension as required for manual models (ATD A on the automatic model).
- Chain off a few stitches.

PREPARING THE NECK

- Place the bias binding along the back of the neckline, right sides together. Allow the binding to extend 2cm (¾in) beyond the shoulders.
- Hold in place with clips and sew.
- Turn the binding to the inside. Iron to hold in place.
- Iron the hem of the front neck inwards (the hem must be as wide at the bias binding). You can clip round the curve to ensure it sits flat.

SEWING THE TOP TOGETHER

- Place the front on the back, right sides together. The hems for the shoulders should measure the same. Tack/baste the front and back hems into place (the neckline is sewn later at the same time as the other hems).
- Slip the seam binding into the presser foot. Use the left needle to make the binding more secure.
- Sew the shoulders with the seam binding. Hide the ends of the threads by weaving them back through the overlock, stitching with a darning needle around the neck. Do not weave them in at the shoulder because these threads will be cut when the top of the sleeves are sewn in.
- Check which is the front and which is the back of the top of the sleeves. The sleeves are not symmetrical.

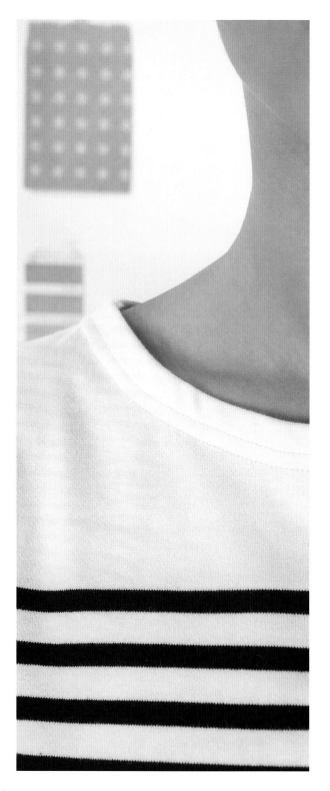

> Hold in place with clips or tack/baste the edge of the sleeves to the armholes, right sides together. Sew together using a 4-thread mock safety stitch.

> Place the front of the top on the back, folding the sleeve in two. Secure in place with clips or tacking/basting stitches to make sure the stripes line up and to stop the fabric from moving. Stitch the sleeve and the side in one go from the bottom of the top to the end of the sleeve.

PREPARING THE HEMS AND NECK

COVERLOCKER SETTINGS
- **Coverstitch**
- **Differential: 1.3**
- **Thread the looper with fluorescent yellow**
- **Thread the two needles (right and left) with fluorescent yellow**

ATTACHING RIBBING

> Fold 2cm (¾in) of fabric inwards for each hem. Iron to keep the fold and to make a slight mark on the right side.

> Use a water-soluble marker pen to draw the mark from the wrong side on to the right side. When you are more used to the machine, you will just need to follow the guide marks on the machine itself.

> Sew round the neckline using a 2-needle coverstitch.

> Sew round the bottom of the garment using the same stitch. The cuffs will be more delicate to sew; take it slowly. Finish the hem precisely at the point where you started it.

Tip

I did not need to adjust the differential much for this fabric as it is a thick jersey that is not overly stretchy. However, if you are using a more stretchy fabric you can do a stitch test. Remember that the stretch of jersey fabric is not the same in both directions (warp and weft) so make sure you perform identical tests throughout.

Attaching bias binding to the back of the neckline

1▸ Place the bias binding along the back of the neckline, right sides together. The bias binding must be longer than the neckline, so it can be sewn on to the front. Because the bias binding does not stretch, the neckline will keep its shape. We will not put bias binding on the front of the neckline to make sure the jersey stays soft around the neckline so you can get it over your head. Hold in place with small clips.

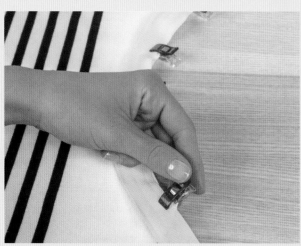

2▸ Beginners can tack/baste the bias binding in place near the edge using white thread. By tacking/basting with white thread, the bias binding can be well positioned and you won't need to unpick the thread because it will be hidden in the seam.

3▸ Overlock the bias binding with the cutter engaged: this gives a neat finish.

4▸ Turn the bias binding to the inside. Iron in place.

Attaching a sleeve

1▸ Stitch the shoulder seams using seam binding.

2▸ Check which is the front and the back of the top of the sleeves. The sleeves are not symmetrical. You could write 'front' and 'back' on them in water-soluble marker pen.

3▸ Line up and clip together the tops of the sleeves and the armholes, right sides together. Then stitch together.

4▸ Place the front of the top on the back of the top, folding the sleeve in half. Secure in place with little clips to make sure the stripes line up. Sew the sleeve and the the side in one seam from the bottom of the top to the end of the sleeve. The threads of the previous seams will be trimmed by the cutter.

Project 8

SIZES: FROM 8 TO 14 (US 4 TO 10)
SHEET A
SEAM ALLOWANCE NOT INCLUDED
3 PIECES
MACHINES USED: OVERLOCKER AND COVERLOCKER

Skirt with elasticated waist

YOU WILL NEED

- 100 x 140cm (39½ x 55in) very thick black jersey fabric
- 70cm (27½in) of 2.5cm (1in) wide elastic ribbon
- 4 reels or cones of black thread
- Standard sewing-box accessories

INSTRUCTIONS

- The skirt will be sewn using a 4-thread mock safety stitch. Sew a stitch sample. Measure stitch width.
- Copy the pattern adding a seam allowance (width of stitch plus about 5mm/¼in) along all seams.
- Add 2cm (¾in) for the hem.
- Cut a front, two backs and a waistband from the fabric, ensuring the grain of the fabric runs in the right direction. Making sure that the grain is in the right direction is essential for the skirt to fall properly.

OVERLOCKER SETTINGS

- Overlock: 4-stitch mock safety
- Differential: 1.5 as the fabric is stretchy
- Cutter: activated
- Stitch finger: N (Neutral) or S (Overlock) depending on model
- Stitch with 2 needles, right and left
- Stitch length N
- Thread the 4 black threads in the correct order (upper looper and lower loop, then right needle followed by left needle)
- Increase presser foot pressure as the fabric is thick

Skirt with elasticated waist

- Sew a short chain of stitches. Do some sample stitching with offcut material, trying out different thicknesses. Adjust the thread tension as required for manual models (ATD A on the automatic model).

- If the fabric is very thick, you may have to change the pressure of the presser foot so that the layers are properly held in place when sewing.

- Sew a short chain of stitches.

- Assemble the two back pieces, right sides together. Hold in place with little clips. Sew together using a 4-thread mock safety stitch.

- Attach the front to the back along the sides, right sides together, using the clips. Sew together using a 4-thread mock safety stitch.

PREPARING THE WAISTBAND

- Fold the waistband in half lengthways, right sides together. Sew the short edges together using a 4-thread mock safety stitch.

- Place the waistband on the top of the skirt, right sides together. Fit the elastic round your waist to check length. Cut off any excess. Fold the elastic in half. Sew into a circle. Place the elastic over the waistband.

- Fold the waistband over the top of the skirt and the elastic. Ensure the waistband is spaced evenly and hold in place with clips. You can also tack/baste the waistband in place – this will make it much easier to stitch later. Tack/baste with a black thread so the stitches will not be seen once the seam has been stitched.

- Sew through the two layers of the waistband and the top of the skirt using a 4-thread mock safety overlock.

Skirt with elasticated waist

PREPARING THE HEM

COVERLOCKER SETTINGS FOR COVERSTITCH

If you have a combi overlocker/coverlocker, set the machine to coverlocker (see Lesson 32, page 116)
- Install the 2 coverlocker needles
- Thread the looper and the needles
- Set the differential to 1.3

› Turn up 2cm (¾in) round the bottom of the skirt. Iron the fold. Ironing the hem will leave a slight mark on the right side of the material.

› Stitch right round. Stop as soon as you get back to where you started so you don't sew over the previous stitches. Tie a knot on the reverse side.

Preparing an elasticated waistband

1▸ Fold the waistband in half lengthways, right sides together, and sew the short ends together using a 4-thread mock safety stitch. Sew the short ends of the elastic together in the same way, having checked the length round your waist.

2▸ Place the waistband on top of the skirt, right sides together. Ensure that the waistband is evenly spaced and hold in place using little clips.

3▸ Slip the elastic over the waistband.

4▸ Fold the waistband back on itself so the elastic is inside the waistband. Hold in place with small clips. Sew through the two layers of the waistband and the top of the skirt using a 4-thread mock safety overlock.

SIZES: FROM 8 TO 14 (US 4 TO 10)
SHEET A
SEAM ALLOWANCE NOT INCLUDED
6 PIECES
MACHINES USED: CONVENTIONAL SEWING MACHINE,
OVERLOCKER, COVERLOCKER

Floral print playsuit

YOU WILL NEED

- 110 x 140cm (43¼ x 55in) blue floral print
- 3 reels or cones of white thread
- 1 reel of navy blue thread
- 1 reel of elastic thread
- 1 piece of grey and silver patterned flat elastic, 2.5cm (1in) wide
- Standard sewing-box accessories

Worth knowing

There are two schools of thought about overlocking garments: some overlock the pieces one by one after cutting them out, then sew them together. Others prefer to tack/baste them together, try on and then sew and overlock the two thicknesses after fitting. A lot depends on the type of material. Some fabric, such as wool or faux fur, can fray, so it's best to overlock them as quickly as possible.

INSTRUCTIONS

› Copy the pattern adding a 1cm (½in) seam allowance. As the seams are made on the sewing machine, you don't need to calculate the allowance. Add 3cm (1¼in) for the bottom hem.

› Cut the top front, the top back, two front legs, two back legs, two pocket fronts and two pocket backs ensuring that the grain of the fabric is in the right direction.

OVERLOCKER SETTINGS

- Overlock stitch: 2-thread
- Differential: 1 or N (Neutral) because the fabric is not stretchy
- Cutter: activated
- Stitch finger: N (Neutral) or S (Overlock) depending on model
- Sew with the right needle for a finer overlock
- Stitch length: 2
- Thread 2 white threads, following the threading order of looper then needle
- Disengage the other looper using the clutch button

› Sew a short chain of stitches. Stitch a sample. Adjust the thread tension as required for manual models (tension E on the automatic model).

› Sew a short chain of stitches. Overlock each piece.

PREPARING THE TOP OF THE PLAYSUIT: STAGE 1

‣ Align the sides of the front and back of the top, right sides together. Use the sewing machine to stitch them together, 1cm (½in) from the edge.

THE LEGS

Place the pocket fronts on the front leg pieces, right sides together, lining up the curved edges. Use the sewing machine to sew along the curve, 1cm (½in) from the edge. Turn each pocket the right way out. Iron in the folds.

OVERLOCKER SETTINGS
- Tight rolled hem stitch: 2-thread
- Differential: Neutral or 1
- Cutter: deactivated
- Stitch finger: R
- Thread the blue threads; follow the threading order of looper then right needle
- Make sure the looper clutch is in place
- Stitch width: 1

‣ Sew a short chain of stitches. Stitch a sample on an offcut of the material. Adjust the thread tension as required for manual models (ATD, D on the automatic model).

‣ Sew a short chain of stitches.

‣ Sew a 2-thread rolled hem along the folded edge.

‣ Keep the settings, activate the cutter and sew a rolled hem round the upper edge of the top.

‣ Place the pocket back and front, right sides together. Sew them together with the sewing machine. Position the pocket in place. Iron.

‣ Place the two front leg pieces right sides together. Use the sewing machine to sew them together around the crotch.

‣ Place the two back leg pieces right sides together. Use the sewing machine to sew them together around the crotch.

‣ Place the front leg piece on the back leg piece, right sides together. Use the sewing machine to sew the sides together.

‣ Hem the bottom of the shorts. Turn up 1cm (½in). Iron to mark the crease. Turn up another 2cm (¾in). Iron. Use the sewing machine to sew the hem.

‣ Thread a gathering thread round the whole of the top of the shorts.

PREPARING THE TOP OF THE PLAYSUIT: STAGE 2

COVERLOCKER SETTINGS
- Chain stitch
- Fit the middle needle
- Thread the looper with elastic thread
- Thread the needle with navy blue thread
- Elastic thread tension: 0

‣ The gathers are sewn with elastic thread in the looper. Do a test run; it is very specific stitching.

‣ Sew chain stitches all round the top, 2cm (¾in) from the edge, with the right side of the stitching face up. Sew a line of chain stitches every 1cm (½in) for about 10cm (4in).

‣ Knot the threads on the back.

‣ Thread two gathering threads round the whole of the bottom part.

ATTACHING THE TOP TO THE BOTTOM

‣ Sew the elastic into a circle. Make sure it is securely attached by using a sewing machine (use a zigzag stitch or oversew several times).

‣ Mark the halfway and quarterway points on the elastic with clips.

COVERLOCKER SETTINGS

- Coverstitch
- Differential: Neutral
- Fit the two coverlocker needles
- Thread the looper and needles with white thread

‣ Mark the halfway and quarterway points on the shorts with clips.

‣ Place the bottom edge of the elastic on the right side of the top of the shorts.

‣ Line up the halfway and quarterway points, and gather evenly using the gathering threads. Tack/baste to ensure the elastic is evenly positioned at the top of the legs.

‣ Sew using coverstitch with the right side of the material face up.

‣ Sew with one needle on the elastic and one on the fabric. Stop stitching when you get to where you started.

‣ Place the top of the elastic on the bottom of the gathered top. Coverstitch in the same way, one needle on the fabric, one on the elastic.

Worth knowing

The tricky bit about this project is the fit: if you pull the waist elastic too tight you will not be able to get it over your hips. Make sure you choose a very stretchy elastic! Try it out first: cut a length of elastic that will go round your hips. Try it round your hips, pulling on it gently but not to its full extent so there is still some give in it.

What is a looper clutch?

1▸ The looper clutch is a small part that is removable on some models and not on others. It is used on overlockers for stitches that need only one looper (chain stitch and 2-thread overlock). When in place, it blocks the upper looper during stitching.

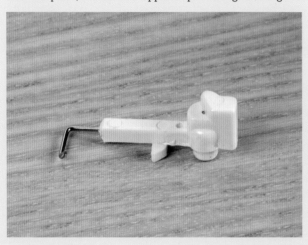

2 ▸ Insert the looper clutch in place.

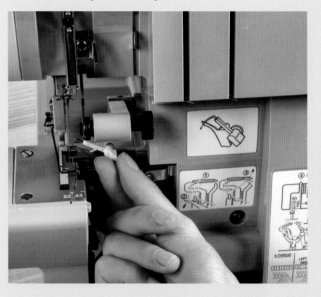

3 ▸ Example of the engaged looper clutch (model 14 T 968 DC).

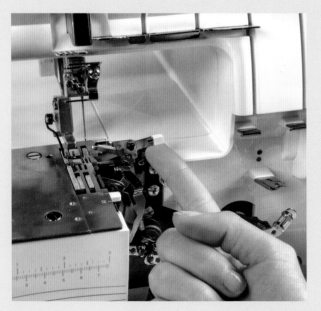

4 ▸ Stitch using a 2-thread overlock. The stitch is finer, and is good for fragile or fine fabrics.

Attaching a pocket

1▶ Place each pocket front on the front side of the shorts, right sides together. Use a conventional sewing machine to sew along the curve, 1cm (½in) from the edge.

2▶ Turn each pocket the right way out. Press in the fold by creasing it by hand, then ironing it.

3▶ Place the pocket back on the pocket, right sides together. Sew them together with the sewing machine. Fold the bottom of the pocket inside. Iron.

4▶ Stitch a rolled hem round the curve, on the right side of the pocket.

Converting the overlocker to coverlocker mode

(only if you are using the 5 - thread 14 J 968 DC model)

1▸ Use the clutch to disengage the upper looper.

2▸ Turn off the machine before you change the lower looper.

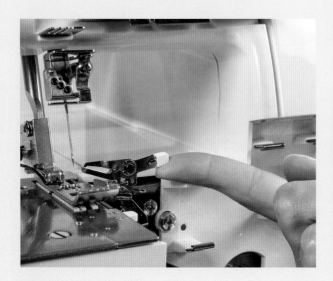

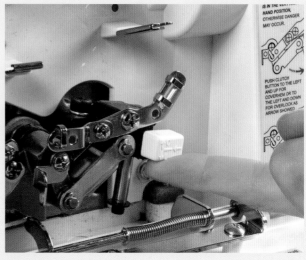

3▸ Disengage the cutter. Change the needle locations (front row). Change the cover.

4▸ Put into R mode (Coverlocker and Rolled).

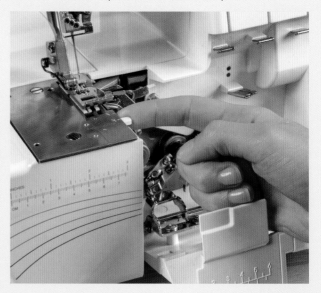

Chain stitch gathers

1▶ On the wrong side of the fabric, use a water-soluble marker pen to draw the first line of gathers 2cm (¾in) from the edge.

2▶ Draw a second parallel line, 1cm (½in) away.

3▶ The gathers are sewn with elastic thread in the looper. It is difficult to thread elastic thread through the needle, so use the threader.
Reduce the looper thread tension as far as possible, in this case to 0, to allow the thick thread to feed through.

4▶ Stitch parallel lines following the guide lines.

SIZES: FROM 8 TO 14 (US 4 TO 10)
SHEET A
SEAM ALLOWANCE NOT INCLUDED
3 PIECES
MACHINES USED: CONVENTIONAL SEWING MACHINE,
OVERLOCKER, COVERLOCKER

Leggings with a bow

YOU WILL NEED

- 70 x 140cm (27½ x 55in) thick grey
  jersey fabric
- 70cm (27½in) black flat elastic
- 70cm (27½in) of 4cm (1½in) wide
  satin ribbon
- 4 reels or cones of black thread
- Standard sewing-box accessories

INSTRUCTIONS

› The leggings will be sewn using a 4-thread mock safety stitch.
Sew a stitch sample. Measure the stitch width.

› Copy the pattern adding a seam allowance (width of stitch plus about
5mm/¼in) along all seams. Add 2cm (¾in) to the bottom of the legs for
the hem.

› Cut the two front leg pieces, two back leg pieces and a waistband from the
fabric, ensuring the grain of the fabric runs in the right direction.

OVERLOCKER SETTINGS
- Overlock: 4-stitch mock safety
- Differential: 1.5 as the fabric is stretchy
- Cutter: activated
- Stitch finger: N (Neutral) or S (Overlock) depending on model
- Stitch with 2 needles, right and left
- Stitch length: N
- Thread the 4 black threads in the correct order (upper looper and lower
  looper, then right needle followed by left needle)

› Sew a short chain of stitches. Do some sample stitching with two layers of
jersey. Adjust the thread tension as required for manual models (ATD A on the
automatic model).

› Sew a short chain of stitches.

Leggings with a bow

PREPARING THE DARTS

› On the wrong side of the back of the legs, mark the darts in white chalk (you won't see marker pen). Prepare, then sew the darts on the sewing machine.

ASSEMBLING THE LEGGINGS

› Assemble the two leg backs by placing one on top of the other, right sides together. Hold in place with small clips or tack/baste together.

› Sew the back crotch on the overlocker using a 4-thread mock safety stitch (see page 28).

› Place the two front leg pieces right sides together. Sew the front crotch on the overlocker using a 4-thread mock safety stitch.

› Place the front leg pieces on the back leg pieces, right sides together. Sew the sides and between the legs on the overlocker using a 4-thread mock safety stitch.

SEWING ON THE WAISTBAND

› Sew the short ends of the waistband with right sides together to make a circle, using a 4-thread mock safety stitch.

› Match the top edge of the waistband with the top edge of the leggings right sides together, placing the seam at the back. Hold in place with small clips.

› Pass the elastic round your waist to check the length. Cut off any excess. Fold the elastic in half and sew the short sides together to make a circle.

› Place the elastic on the waistband. Fold the bottom half of the waistband up and over the elastic and secure with clips. Unless you are feeling very confident, tack/baste the waistband into place. This will make the stitching much easier.

› Sew together using a 4-thread mock safety stitch.

› Tie a bow with the satin ribbon. Sew the bow to the top of the back seam.

PREPARING THE BOTTOM HEM

COVERLOCKER SETTINGS

- Coverstitch
- Install the two coverlocker needles
- Thread the needles
- Thread the looper
- Differential:1.3

› Try the leggings on for length. Trim if the legs are too long, leaving a 2cm (¾in) hem allowance.

› Turn up 2cm (¾in) round the bottom of the legs. Iron the fold to make a slight mark on the right side of the fabric to give you a stitch line.

› Place the bottom of the turned-up legs on the machine, right side up. You can no longer see the turn-up. It is not easy to sew coverstitch hems round small openings like these. You need to take your time and sew little by little, turning the fabric before continuing the seam.

› Sew right round on the outside of the bottom of each leg. Stop as soon as you get back to the start so you don't sew over the previous stitches. Tie a knot on the reverse side.

Worth knowing

You can also sew the front and back of each leg along the sides. Then sew the hem using coverstitch before sewing up each leg. The coverstitching will be easier but this method does not give you the opportunity to fit the length.

Sewing trousers together

1 ▸ Sew the darts on the sewing machine.

2 ▸ Place the two back pieces right sides together. Sew around the crotch on the overlocker using a 4-thread safety stitch.

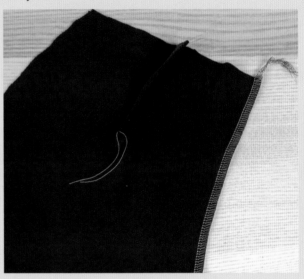

3 ▸ Place the two front pieces right sides together. Sew the crotch.

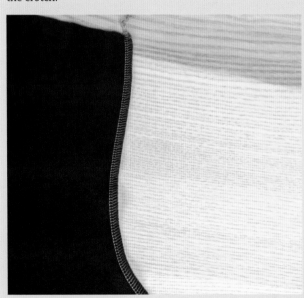

4 ▸ Place the front on the back, right sides together. Sew up the sides, still using the 4-thread safety stitch (then stitch right round both inside legs in one go).

Making seams less bulky

1 ▸ Hold the layers to be stitched in place with clips. Sew the first seam in one direction, then the next seam in the opposite direction.

2 ▸ Stitch, making sure the seams do not overlap.

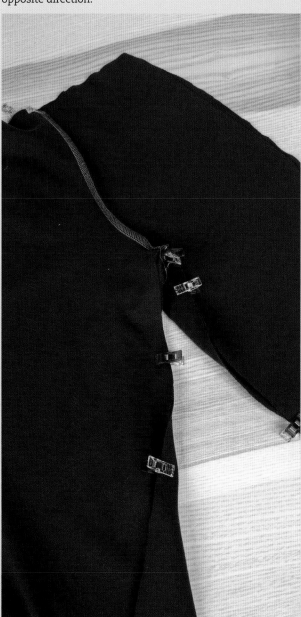

SIZES: FROM 8 TO 14 (US 4 TO 10)
SHEET B
SEAM ALLOWANCE NOT INCLUDED
3 PIECES
MACHINES USED: OVERLOCKER AND COVERLOCKER

Dress with a waistband

YOU WILL NEED

- 120 x 140cm (47½ x 55in) polo-style blue jersey fabric
- 70cm (27½in) of 5cm (2in) wide patterned elastic
- 4 reels or cones of dark blue thread
- 30cm (11¾in) of black seam binding for the shoulders
- 30cm (11¾in) of 4mm ($^3/_{16}$in) wide elastic ribbon
- Standard sewing-box accessories

Worth knowing

To save time, you could make this with a fitted T-shirt bought from a shop.

INSTRUCTIONS

› The seams will be sewn using a 4-thread mock safety stitch. Sew a sample. Measure the stitch width. Copy the pattern adding a seam allowance (width of stitch plus about 5mm/¼in) along the front and back sides, the cuffs, the tops of the sleeves and the neckline. The bottoms of the sleeves do not have a seam or hem, so need to be cut in accordance with the pattern.

› Cut a front, back and two sleeves from the fabric, ensuring the grain of the fabric runs in the right direction. Cut a 6 x 60cm (2½ x 23¾in) band for the neck. Cut a 50 x 140cm (19¾ x 55in) rectangle (width of fabric) for the skirt.

OVERLOCKER SETTINGS

- Overlock: 4-thread mock safety stitch
- Differential: 1.3 as the fabric is stretchy
- Cutter: activated
- Stitch finger: N (Neutral) or S (Overlock) depending on model
- Stitch with 2 needles, right and left
- Stitch length: N
- Thread the 4 black threads in the correct order (upper looper and lower looper, then right needle followed by left needle)

› Sew a stitch chain. Sew a stitch sample. Adjust thread tension as required (ATD A on the automatic model).

› Sew a short chain of stitches.

Dress with a waistband

PREPARING THE T-SHIRT

‣ Place the back piece on the front, right sides together. Slip the seam binding under the presser foot. Sew the shoulders together using a 4-thread mock safety stitch. Sew the two shoulders together in one go. Cut the binding and the threads between the two shoulders so they are separate again.

PREPARING THE NECK

‣ Fold the neckband lengthways, with right sides together, to form a circle. Sew together using a 4-thread mock safety stitch. Iron. Fold the band widthways and sew together using a 4-thread mock safety stitch. Iron.

‣ Mark the halfway and quarterway points of the neckband with clips.

‣ Mark the halfway and quarterway points of the neckline with clips.

‣ Place the neckband round the neckline, right sides together, lining up the markers.

‣ Stitch together increasing the differential to 1.5 and using a 4-thread safety stitch, placing the neck against the feed dogs.

PREPARING THE BOTTOM OF THE SLEEVES

‣ Fit the presser foot for elastic.

OVERLOCKER SETTINGS
- **Overlock stitch: 3-thread safety stitch, left needle**
- **Cutter: activated**
- **Differential: 1.5**

‣ Do some test stitching with an offcut of the material and a piece of elastic. Adjust the tensions if necessary.

‣ Put two marker darts into the bottom of the sleeves (see pattern).

‣ Position the elastic in the presser foot.

‣ Sew the bottom of the sleeve with the elastic. Stretch the elastic (using the special knob at the top of the presser foot) between the pinned markers. This will ensure that the bottom of this sleeve is well formed and slightly puffed.

ATTACHING THE SLEEVES TO THE DRESS

OVERLOCKER SETTINGS
- **Overlock: 4-stitch mock safety**
- **Install the gathering foot**
- **Cutter: activated**

‣ If you are using a manual model, perform a stitch test and adjust the tensions as required.

‣ Place the fabric of the sleeve under the presser foot first, with the wrong side against the feed dogs. Don't forget, with the gathering foot, the fabric to be gathered should be underneath, against the feed dogs. You can raise the presser foot to make sure the fabric is being properly held in place.

‣ Place the sleeve hole open on the top of the sleeve under the presser foot, right sides together. Sew around the top of the sleeve using a 4-thread mock safety stitch.

‣ Attach the second sleeve in the same way.

ASSEMBLING THE T-SHIRT

‣ Place the T-shirt front on the T-shirt back, right sides together. The sleeves are folded in half.

‣ Sew one side together, from the bottom of the sleeve to the bottom of the T-shirt in a single seam, using a 4-thread mock safety overlock with the differential set to 1.3.

PREPARING THE SKIRT

‣ Thread two gathering threads round the top of the skirt. Sew the gathering thread by hand or using a conventional sewing machine set to long stitches. Pull gently on the gathering stitches to reduce the width of the skirt to that of the T-shirt.

COVERLOCKER SETTINGS

- Fit the two coverlocker needles
- Thread the looper, then the needles
- Differential: 1.5

SEWING TOGETHER THE T-SHIRT AND THE SKIRT

‣ Fit the elastic round your waist. Cut off any excess. Mark the halfway and quarterway points of the circle on the skirt and the elastic with clips. Place the bottom edge of the elastic on the right side of the the skirt top, lining up the clips. Gather evenly using the gathering threads. Tack/baste the elastic to the skirt top.

‣ Coverstitch, with the wrong side of the skirt against the machine and the right side face up. Sew with one needle on the elastic and one on the fabric.

‣ Place the top of the elastic on the bottom of the T-shirt. Coverstitch in the same way, one needle on the fabric, one needle on the elastic, with the right side of the dress face up.

‣ Sew up the second side of the dress. Sew up the non-sewn side, right sides together, from the bottom of the sleeve to the bottom of the skirt in one go.

HEMMING THE DRESS

‣ Turn the bottom of the skirt up 4cm (1½in) inwards. Iron the hem to make a slight mark on the right side of the fabric. This gives you a stitch guide. Try on the skirt. To make it shorter, put in a larger hem.

‣ Place the wrong side of the skirt on the machine, right side up. You can no longer see the turn-up.

‣ Stitch right round. Stop stitching as soon as you get back to the beginning so you don't sew over the previous stitches. Tie a knot on the wrong side.

Attaching a neckband

1▸ Fold the neckband right sides together lengthways to form a tube. Sew together using a 4-thread mock safety overlock.

2▸ Fold the band widthways. Sew together using a 4-thread mock safety stitch. Iron.

3▸ Find the halfway and quarterway points along the band. Mark with clips.
Find the halfway and quarterway points round the neck. Mark with clips.
Place the hemmed edge of the band round the neck, right sides together, stretching slightly so that it will be a little tighter at the fold. Line up the markers.

4▸ Ensure the neck is turned down on to the T-shirt so the bottom edge of the neck is free; this will make stitching easier. Stitch together.

Gathering and attaching a sleeve with the gathering foot

1▸ Sew the shoulders using seam binding in a single seam. Separate the shoulders by cutting the binding.

2▸ Install the gathering foot on the overlocker. This presser foot only gathers the layer of fabric lying on the feed dogs.

3▸ Place the layer that is to be gathered against the feed dogs. Allow a small amount extra for the fabric that is to be gathered; as the fabric is offset, it will be picked up first. Lower the presser foot.

4▸ Feed the second layer between the two blades of the gathering foot. Push against the fabric to make sure it is taken in. Stitch together. As you are stitching, only the bottom layer is gathered.

Stitching on elastic using the special presser foot

1▸ You can leave the cutter in place because the special presser foot slightly offsets the position of the elastic. Only the fabric placed underneath is cut. Pass the elastic into the presser foot.

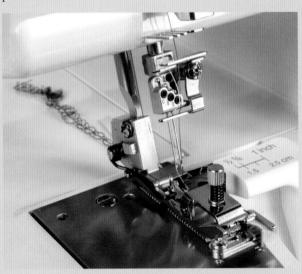

2▸ Set the tension of the elastic using the special knob on top of the presser foot.

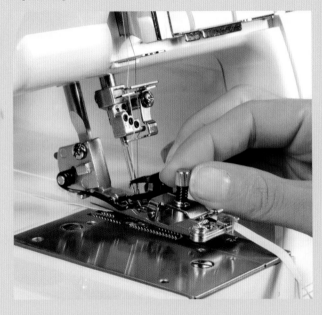

3▸ Slip the fabric under the presser foot, right side on the feed dogs, wrong side facing upwards. Lower the presser foot.

4▸ Sew around the bottom of the sleeve with the elastic using a 4-thread mock safety overlock.

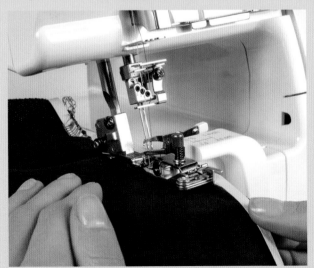

Stitching elastic round the waist using coverstitch

1 ▸ Thread a gathering thread round the top of the skirt.

2 ▸ Thread a second gathering thread, parallel to the first. Pull gently on the threads to gather the fabric.

3 ▸ Mark the halfway and quarterway points of the circle on the skirt and the elastic with clips.
Place the bottom edge of the elastic on the right side of the top of the skirt, ensuring the markers are lined up. Tack/baste so the elastic is accurately positioned at the top of the skirt.
Coverstitch, with the wrong side of the skirt against the machine and the right side face up.

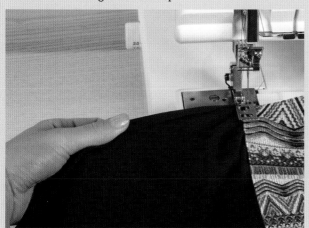

4 ▸ Sew with one needle on the elastic and another on the skirt.

Project 12

SINGLE SIZE
NO PATTERN
MACHINE USED: OVERLOCKER

Pillows

YOU WILL NEED

For the square slate-grey pillow
(35 x 35cm/13¾ x 13¾in)

‣ 40 x 80cm (15¾ x 31½in) thick slate grey
  jersey fabric
‣ 150cm (59in) of mustard-coloured
  pompom braid

For the square grey pillow
(50 x 50cm/19¾ x 19¾in)

‣ 50 x 100cm (19¾ x 39½in) thick grey
  jersey fabric
‣ 210cm (82¾in) of starry piping

For the rectangular mustard-coloured pillow
(20 x 60cm/8 x 23¾in)

‣ 60 x 110cm (23¾ x 43¼in) thick mustard-
  coloured jersey fabric
‣ 180cm (71in) of blue pompom braid

FOR EACH PILLOW

‣ A bag of cotton or synthetic-fibre
  stuffing material
‣ 3 reels or cones of matching thread
‣ A special piping presser foot
‣ Standard sewing-box accessories

INSTRUCTIONS

‣ Cut the shape of the pillow twice from the fabric. For jersey fabrics, it is sometimes useful to draw the shape before you cut as the fabric tends to slide around.

OVERLOCKER SETTINGS

- Overlock stitch: 3-thread
- Attach the special piping presser foot
- Differential: 1.5 as the fabric is stretchy
- Cutter: activated
- Stitch finger: N (Neutral) or S (Overlock) depending on model
- Sew with the right needle for a narrower stitch
- Stitch length: N
- Thread the 3 threads in the correct order (upper looper and lower loop, then needle)

‣ Sew a short chain of stitches.

‣ Do some test stitching with two layers of jersey fabric. Adjust the thread tension as required for manual models (ATD A on the automatic model).

‣ Chain off.

› Stitching piping or braid between two pieces of fabric on the overlocker is done in the same way as on a conventional sewing machine:

   - Sew the braid or piping all round the pillow, on the right side, with the decorative edge towards the inside of the pillow.

   - At the corners, ensure the needle is right down through the fabric, lift the presser foot and rotate the fabric 90°.

› Swap the presser foot for the standard presser foot.

OVERLOCKER SETTINGS

   - Adjust the thread tension again, as there are now more layers

   - Disengage the cutter so you don't damage the stitching you have already done

   - Increase presser foot tension slightly to ensure that the layers of fabric are held firmly in place during stitching

› Place the second pillow piece on the first, right sides together. Position the piece with the piping seam facing you. Sew over the previous seam. Sew round the four sides, leaving approximately 15cm (6in) open.

› Carefully stuff the pillow.

› Turn in slightly along both sides of the opening. Oversew the opening closed by hand.

Changing a presser foot

1▶ Raise the presser foot.

2▶ Unclip the presser foot (using the knob behind).

3▶ Insert the new presser foot. You need to slide it under the locking bar.

4▶ Lower the presser-foot bar. Press the knob down to lock into place.

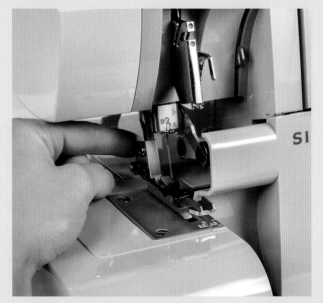

Stitching on braid using the special presser foot

1▸ Attach the special braid or piping presser foot. Insert the braid in the zip guide, with the decorative edge facing towards the inside of the pillow.

2▸ Stitch the braid right round the pillow, on the right side of the fabric. The braid is positioned by the presser foot in such a way that it is not cut. However, the fabric placed on top will be trimmed by the cutter.

3▸ At the corners, make sure the needle is down and through all the layers. Lift the presser foot, turn the fabric, lower the presser foot and continue stitching.

4▸ Swap the presser foot for the standard presser foot. Place the second piece of fabric on top of the first. Line up the seams and deactivate the cutter. Increase presser foot tension slightly to ensure the layers of fabric are held firmly in place during stitching.

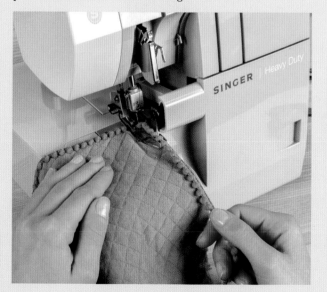

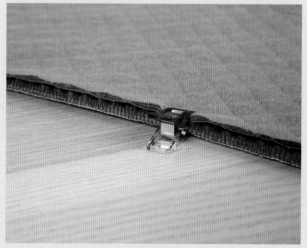

Project 13

SIZES: FROM 8 TO 14 (US 4 TO 10)
SHEET A
SEAM ALLOWANCE NOT INCLUDED
1 PIECE
MACHINES USED: OVERLOCKER AND COVERLOCKER

T-shirt with decorative seams

YOU WILL NEED

‣ 80 x 140cm (31½ x 55in) thin ivory-coloured jersey fabric
‣ 4 reels or cones of ivory-coloured thread
‣ 2 cones of woolly nylon thread
‣ 1 reel of gold thread
‣ 60cm (23¾in) of seam binding for the shoulders
‣ Standard sewing-box accessories

INSTRUCTIONS

‣ The T-shirt is sewn using a 4-thread safety stitch. Sew a stitch sample. Measure the stitch width.

‣ Copy the pattern, adding a seam allowance (width of stitch plus about 5mm/¼in) along the sides, shoulders and neckline.

‣ For the hems, add 2.5cm (1in) at the bottom of the front and back pieces and the bottom of the sleeves.

‣ Cut a front and back from the fabric, ensuring the grain of the fabric is in the right direction.

‣ Cut a 6 x 65cm (2½ x 25½in) band for the neck.

PREPARING THE T-SHIRT

OVERLOCKER SETTINGS

- Overlock: 4-stitch mock safety
- Differential: 1.3, as the fabric is stretchy
- Cutter: activated
- Stitch finger: N (Neutral) or S (Overlock) depending on model
- Stitch with 2 needles, right and left
- Stitch length: N
- Thread the 4 ivory threads in the correct order (upper looper and lower looper, then right needle followed by left needle)

T-shirt with decorative seams

‣ Sew a short chain of stitches.

‣ Stitch a sample. Adjust the thread tension as required (tension A on the automatic model).

‣ Sew a short chain of stitches.

‣ Slip the seam binding into the presser foot. Place the front on the back, right sides together. Line up the shoulders. Stitch the shoulders together, taking the seam binding into the seam. The presser foot positions the binding in such a way that it won't cut it. Stitch one shoulder then the other as if they were the same seam.

‣ Cut the stitches and the seam binding between the two shoulders.

‣ To make the seam softer, thread the loopers with the woolly nylon thread. To do this, you will need to rethread all the threads in the correct order (upper looper and lower looper, then the needles).

‣ Sew the sides, right sides together, using a 4-thread mock safety stitch. Check the differential. As the jersey is only sewn in the same direction on the shoulders, it is possible you might have to adjust the differential slightly. You don't need to make any further adjustments.

PREPARING THE NECK

› Sew the neckband into a circle by folding it in half lengthways, right sides together, using a 4-thread mock safety stitch. Fold the band in half widthways with right sides out.

› Mark the halfway and quarterway points with clips round the base of the neck. Mark the halfway and quarterway points with clips round the neckline of the T-shirt.

› Place the base of the neck round the neckline and stretch it to line up the markers, otherwise the T-shirt will stretch under the weight of the fabric.

› Set the differential to 1.5. Sew round the neck using a 4-thread mock safety overlock, with the neck against the machine's feed dogs.

› 4cm (1½in) from the end of the seam, disengage the cutter. This is important, otherwise you will cut off the beginning of the seam.

PREPARING THE HEMS

› Turn up the bottoms of the sleeves and the bottom of the T-shirt by 1cm (½in) then 2cm (¾in). Tack/baste with the ivory thread.

SETTING UP THE COVERLOCKER WITH THE GOLD THREAD

COVERLOCKER SETTINGS
- Insert the 3 needles. Slightly unscrew the 3 needles before you insert them and then retighten them
- Thread the looper with gold thread
- Thread the needles with the ivory thread
- Decrease the looper thread tension (tension very loose)
- So that the looper thread is visible, stitch wrong side face up, with one needle on each side of the fold

› Place the neck wrong side up under the presser foot. Sew using a 3-needle coverstitch, with the gold thread in the looper, round the whole seam of the neck assembly.

› Sew the hems of the sleeves in the same way as the neck, using a 3-needle coverstitch to achieve the same effect.

› Turn the T-shirt right side out. Trim the neck. Cut along the neck fold by sliding a blade of some scissors into the neck. Allow the edges to roll themselves up.

PREPARING THE BOTTOM HEM

The bottom hem is sewn in a more classic style using a 3-thread coverstitch and the ivory looper thread.

› Turn up 2.5cm (1in) to the inside. Iron. You can trace the line from the reverse side on to the right side of the fabric using a water-soluble marker pen, or the T-shirt may be sufficiently transparent to see it anyway. Sew round using a 3-needle overlock.

Stitching with woolly nylon thread

1▸ Only thread the woolly nylon thread in the loopers. Woolly nylon thread is very elastic and very soft. It is perfect for ensuring that seams do not irritate.

2▸ Place the back on the front, right sides together. Hold in place with small clips.

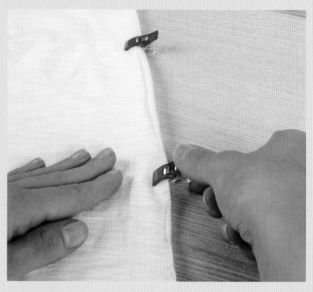

3▸ Stitch the sleeve and one side in a single seam. Remove the clips before they get to the presser foot.

4▸ The seam will be soft and stretchy.

Sewing a double neck

1▶ Sew the shoulders using seam binding. Stitch the two shoulders together with a single seam. Cut the binding to separate the shoulders.

2▶ Place the neck on the neckline, ensuring that you stretch the neck as required.

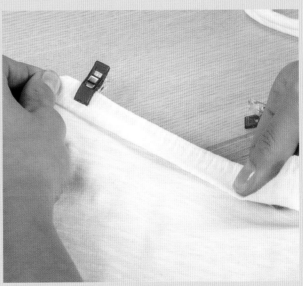

3▶ Stitch on the neck using the overlocker.

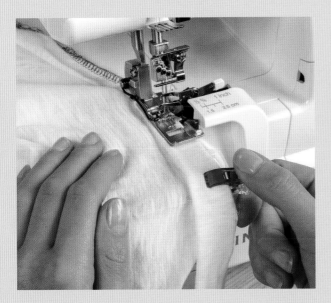

4▶ Slide the blade of the scissors into the neck. Cut the neck, 1cm (½in) from the edge. Allow the two parts of the neck to roll up.

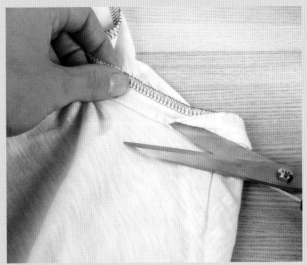

Sewing mock chain stitch with gold thread on the coverlocker

1▶ Insert the 3 needles (slightly unscrew the 3 needles before you insert them and then retighten them). Thread the looper with gold thread. Thread the needles.

2▶ Decrease the looper tension (you need very loose tension so the thread slides easily through the thread guides and doesn't get hooked up).

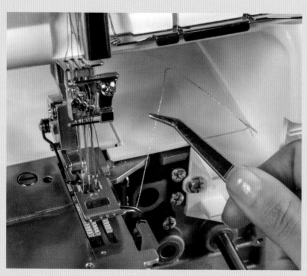

3▶ For the looper thread to show on the right side of the fabric, sew wrong side face up, with one needle on either side of the previous stitchline.

4▶ The gold thread has no stretch in it so the stitching is generally not perfectly even. This is what gives the stitch its 'chain link' effect.

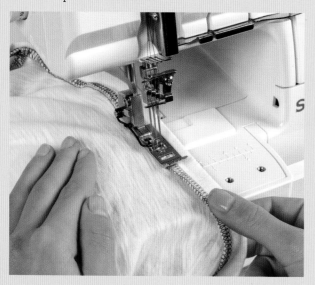

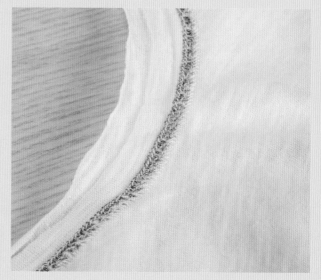

3 – needle coverstitching

1▶ Install the 3 needles on the overlocker. The stitching is going to be very wide.

2▶ Thread the three needles, from right to left.

3▶ Turn up 2.5cm (1in) of the bottom of the T-shirt to the wrong side. Iron.

4▶ Use a water-soluble marker pen to trace the hem line from the reverse side on to the right side. If you can follow the line through the fabric, you can sew without doing this. Stitch with the right side of the fabric face up.

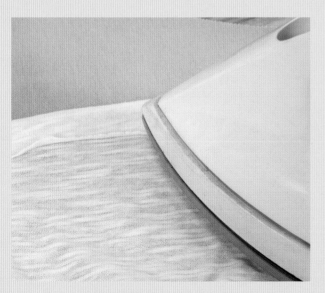

SIZES: FROM 8 TO 14 (US 4 TO 10)
SHEET B
SEAM ALLOWANCE NOT INCLUDED
4 PIECES
MACHINES USED: CONVENTIONAL SEWING MACHINE,
OVERLOCKER AND COVERLOCKER

Jacket with hood

YOU WILL NEED

- › 150 x 140cm (59 x 55in) of polyester fabric with faux fur lining
- › 1 separable 50cm (19¾in) ivory zip fastener
- › 4 reels or cones of ivory-coloured thread
- › 40 x 90cm wide (15¾ x 35½in) ivory ribbing
- › Standard sewing-box accessories

Worth knowing

This is where the overlocker really comes into its own. It is indispensable not just because the faux fur is not stretchy, but also because it requires a really good overlock!

INSTRUCTIONS

› The jacket is sewn using a 4-thread safety stitch. Sew a sample. Measure the stitch width.

› Copy the pattern adding a seam allowance (width of stitch plus about 5mm/¼in) along all seams. The front opening and the front of the hood have no seams, cut as per the pattern.

› Cut two front pieces, a back, two sleeves and two hood pieces from the fabric. Ensure the grain of the fabric runs in the right direction so that all the fur goes the same way. You can vacuum the edge of the pieces to get rid of as much fluff as possible.

› Cut a band from the ribbing for the bottom of the jacket that is 11cm (4¼in) deep and 68cm (26¾in) long, and two 11 x 18cm (4¼ x 7in) bands for the cuffs.

OVERLOCKER SETTINGS

- Overlock: 4-stitch mock safety
- Differential: 1 or N (Neutral) because the fabric does not stretch
- Cutter: deactivated, otherwise you will have lint everywhere
- Stitch finger: N (Neutral) or S (Overlock) depending on model
- Stitch with the two needles
- Stitch length: 2
- Thread the 4 threads in the correct order (upper looper and lower looper, then the needles)

- Chain off.

- Sew a sample. Adjust the thread tension as required (tension A on the automatic model).

- Sew a short chain of stitches.

- Assemble the shoulders, right sides together. Sew together using a 4-thread mock safety stitch.

- Fit the sleeves to the armholes, right sides together. Stitch ensuring you know which is the front and which is the back of the top of the sleeve.

ATTACHING THE RIBBED CUFFS

- For each cuff:

Fold the ribbing lengthways to get a 5.5cm wide (2¼in) band. Stretch the ribbing band round the end of the sleeve. Attach using little clips to the right side of the bottom of the sleeve. Beginners may want to tack/baste on the cuffs in ivory thread to hold them in place.

- Adjust the differential setting (set at 1.5), because the cuffs are stretchy. Place the cuffs against the overlocker feed dogs so that the elasticity can be absorbed by the differential feed. Use a 4-thread mock safety stitch to sew together.

- Return the differential to the neutral position. Fold the jacket so the front is on top of the back and the sleeves are folded (right sides together). Sew the sides together in one long seam from the bottom round to the cuff. Use a 4-thread mock safety stitch to sew together.

ATTACHING RIBBING TO THE BOTTOM OF THE JACKET

- Fold the ribbing lengthways to get a 5.5cm wide (2¼in) band. Stretch the ribbing band round the bottom of the jacket. Attach using little clips to the right side of the bottom of the jacket. The ribbing waistband should start and finish 2cm (¾in) from the front (so that the zip fastener can then be put in). Hold in place using little clips or tack/baste with the ivory thread.

- Adjust the differential setting (set to 1.5), because the band is stretchy.

- Place the ribbing band against the overlocker feed dogs. Use a 4-thread mock safety stitch to sew together.

ATTACHING THE HOOD

- Assemble the two pieces of the hood, right sides together. Hold in place with small clips. Sew together using a 4-thread mock safety stitch (differential at neutral as the fabric is not stretchy).

- Find the middle of the back by folding it in half. Mark the middle with a clip.

- Align the middle of the back and the middle of the hood (seam line), right sides together. Hold in place using little clips or tack/baste the hood into place. Use a 4-thread mock safety stitch to sew round the whole hood.

Jacket with hood

PUTTING IN THE ZIP

› Overlock the whole of the front (including the hood) with a 3-thread overlock. Use a tight stitch to ensure the fabric does not shed (neutral differential).

› Set up a conventional sewing machine. Turn the two front pieces in 2cm (¾in). The ribbing and the front are now aligned.

› Place the closed zip fastener under the turned in edges and check that it is accurately positioned. Tack/baste the zip into place
on each side. Fold the top of the zip binding back on itself to create a neat finish. Tack/baste each side of the zip.

› Unzip the fastener before you stitch it into place. If you have a special presser foot, this is the time to use it. If not, as the zip binding is wide, the normal sewing machine presser foot will do the job.

› Fold back 2cm (¾in) all round the hood so some of the fur is visible. Sew the fold into place by hand.

Sewing with faux fur

1▸ Deactivate the cutter because faux fur frays a lot.

2▸ Use a 4-thread mock safety overlock to keep the seams as tight as possible. Adjust the end so the stitches are very tight.

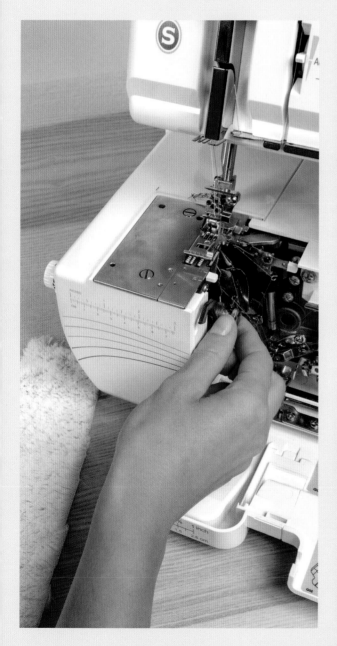

Attaching a hood

1▸ Place the two parts of the hood on top of each other, right sides together, then sew round the curved edge.

2▸ Find the middle of the back piece by folding it in half. Mark the middle with a clip.

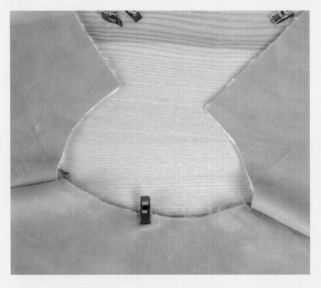

3▸ Align the middle of the back and the middle of the hood (seam line), right sides together.

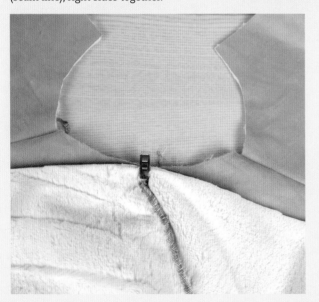

4▸ Hold the hood pieces together with small clips. Use a 4-thread mock safety stitch to sew round the whole hood.

Attaching ribbing cuffs

1▶ Fold the ribbing lengthways to get a 5.5cm-wide (2¼in) band.

2▶ Stretch the ribbing band round the end of the sleeve Attach using little clips to the right side of the bottom of the sleeve.

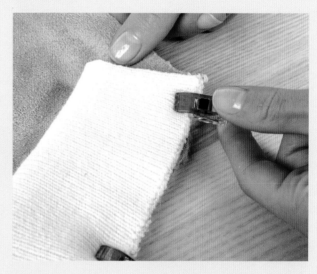

3▶ Adjust the differential setting (set at 1.5), because the cuffs are stretchy.
Place the cuffs on the overlocker feed dogs. Sew together using a 4-thread safety stitch.

4▶ Return the differential to the neutral position. Fold the jacket so the front is on top of the back and the sleeves are folded right sides together. Sew the sides together in one long seam from the bottom round to the cuff. Sew together using a 4-thread mock safety stitch.

Project 15

ONE SIZE
SHEET B
SEAM ALLOWANCE INCLUDED
1 PIECE
MACHINES USED: OVERLOCKER AND COVERLOCKER

Reversible denim and gold bag

YOU WILL NEED

- 40 x 140cm (15¾ x 55in) gold fabric
- 40 x 140cm (15¾ x 55in) fusible webbing
- 100 x 140cm (39½ x 55in) denim fabric
- 5 reels or cones of black thread
- 4 eyelets (with setting kit and hammer)
- 2 large adjustable leather handles
- 4 big rings
- Standard sewing-box accessories
- Iron

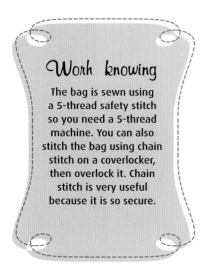

Worth knowing

The bag is sewn using a 5-thread safety stitch so you need a 5-thread machine. You can also stitch the bag using chain stitch on a coverlocker, then overlock it. Chain stitch is very useful because it is so secure.

INSTRUCTIONS

› Copy the pattern. Seam allowances are given on the pattern. (As the bag isn't fitted like a garment, the seam allowance is less important.)

› Cut out the main pieces of the bag twice from the gold fabric to make the front and back.

› Cut out the main pieces of the bag twice from the denim to make the inside of the front and back.

› Cut two 12 x 50cm (4¾ x 19¾in) gussets from the denim (not included on the pattern).

OVERLOCKER-COVERLOCKER SETTINGS

- Overlock: 5-thread safety stitch
- Swap the needles for more solid ones (90)
- Differential: N (Neutral), because the fabrics do
  not stretch
- Cutter: activated
- Stitch finger: N (Neutral) or S (Overlock) depending on model
- Sew with 2 needles, right at the back for the overlock needle and middle at the front for the chain stitch needle
- Stitch length: 2.5 or N
- Thread the 5 threads in the correct order (upper looper and lower looper, chain stitch looper, then needles)

Reversible denim and gold bag

• Chain off. Stitch a sample. Adjust thread tension as required (ATD B on the automatic model).

• Chain off.

• The bag is reversible, therefore you need to sew two bags separately before assembling them. The outside bag is made of gold fabric reinforced with fusible webbing. The sides are denim. The inside bag is made completely of denim.

• Place the fusible webbing on the front and back pieces cut from the gold fabric, wrong sides together. Press with an iron (without steam function) for 10 seconds. Iron all the fabric in this way. Allow it to cool for 5 minutes. Iron again if there are any air bubbles. Allow to cool. Crease the fabric slightly for a textured finish.

ASSEMBLING THE OUTSIDE BAG AND THE LINING BAG SEPARATELY

For each bag:

• Assemble the front piece and gusset right sides together. Hold in place with small clips. You can also tack/baste the bag together, but this may be tricky as the fabric is thick. Stitch using a 5-thread safety overlock or chain stitch then overlock.

• Attach the back along the other long edge of the gusset. Hold in place with small clips. Stitch using a 5-thread safety stitch.

SEWING THE BAG TOGETHER

• Turn the outer bag right side out. Slide the outer bag into the inside bag. The two bags should be right sides together.

• Sew all round the top using a 5-thread overlock, leaving a 10cm (4in) opening.

• Turn the bag through and push the lining bag into the outer bag.

• Sew the opening closed by hand using invisible stitches.

TO FINISH

• Put the eyelets on each side of the top of the bag, 14cm (5½in) from the curved edge and 2cm (¾in) from the top. Attach following the manufacturer's instructions on the eyelet kit.

• Clip the handles to the handle rings.

Setting eyelets

1▶ Mark the position of the eyelets using a tape measure and tailor's chalk.

2▶ Snip the fabric where the eyelets will be.

3▶ Position the two parts of the eyelet, the big piece on the front of the fabric, the smaller piece on the back of the fabric.

4▶ Use the setting kit and hammer to attach the eyelet in place.

Sewing a reversible bag using a 5-thread safety stitch

1▸ Adjust the overlocker-coverlocker. Sew with 2 needles, right back for the overlock needle and middle front for the chain stitch needle. Thread the 5 threads into the loopers and needles. Activate the cutter. Sew the outer bag and the lining bag separately.

2▸ Turn the outer bag right side out. Slide the outer bag into the inner bag. The two bags should be right sides together.

3▸ Use small clips round the top of the two bags to hold them in place.

4▸ Sew all round the top using a 5-thread safety stitch, leaving a 10cm (4in) opening. Turn the bag right side out and push the lining into the outer bag. Sew the opening closed by hand using invisible stitches.

First published in Great Britain in 2018
by Search Press Limited
Wellwood, North Farm Road
Tunbridge Wells, Kent TN2 3DR

Original title: *J'apprends à coudre à la surjeteuse et à la recouvreuse*
© 2016 by Éditions Marie Claire-Société d'Information et de Créations (SIC)

English translation by Burravoe Translation Services

Director of publishing: Thierry Lamarre
Creator and writer: Clémentine Lubin
Editing/proofreading: Isabelle Misery
Photographs: Pierre Nicou
Styling: Émilie Rouffiat
Graphic design and lay-out: Either studio
Cover: Either studio
Thank you to Marie-France Morel (Singer) for her help and advice.
Thanks to France Duval-Stalla for her fabrics.
SINGER Machines
Information and addresses at www.singerfrance.com

ISBN: 978-1-78221-490-8

If you have difficulty in obtaining any of the materials and equipment mentioned
in this book, then please visit the Search Press website for details of suppliers:
www.searchpress.com

Printed in China through Asia Pacific Offset